PLANTS & GARDENS

BROOKLYN BOTANIC GARDEN RECORD

A NEW LOOK AT

Houseplants

1993

Plants & Gardens, Brooklyn Botanic Garden Record (ISSN 0362-5850)

is published quarterly at 1000 Washington Ave., Brooklyn, N.Y. 11225, by the **Brooklyn Botanic Garden, Inc.**

Subscription included in Botanic Garden membership dues ($25.00 per year).

Copyright © 1993 by the Brooklyn Botanic Garden, Inc.

ISBN # 0-945352-81-6

Brooklyn Botanic Garden

STAFF FOR THIS EDITION:

Tovah Martin
GUEST EDITOR

Janet Marinelli
EDITOR

Barbara B. Pesch
DIRECTOR OF PUBLICATIONS
AND THE EDITORIAL COMMITTEE OF THE BROOKLYN BOTANIC GARDEN

Bekka Lindstrom
ART DIRECTOR

Judith D. Zuk
PRESIDENT, BROOKLYN BOTANIC GARDEN

Elizabeth Scholtz
DIRECTOR EMERITUS, BROOKLYN BOTANIC GARDEN

Stephen K-M. Tim
VICE PRESIDENT, SCIENCE & PUBLICATIONS

Front and Back Cover Photographs by Charles Marden Fitch

PLANTS & GARDENS
BROOKLYN BOTANIC GARDEN RECORD

A NEW LOOK

Houseplants

VOL. 49, NO. 4, WINTER 1993

HANDBOOK #137

CONTRIBUTORS

RITA BUCHANAN has written and edited for several garden publications including *Fine Gardening* magazine, the *Herb Companion* and *Taylor's Guides to Gardening*. She is author of *The Weaver's Garden* (Interweave Press, 1987).

WALTER DWORKIN is President of the Brooklyn/Queens/Nassau County, New York, Branch of the American Begonia Society. Walter has been growing begonias for the past 14 years in his Long Island home.

RICHARD EGGENBERGER and his wife Mary Helen are founders of The Plumeria People, a worldwide retail mail-order company specializing in tropical plants. They have published *The Handbook on Plumeria Culture*.

CHARLES MARDEN FITCH has authored numerous books, most recently, *Fresh Flowers: Identifying, Selecting and Arranging* (Abbeville Press, 1992). He has guest edited several BBG handbooks, including *Garden Photography* and *Orchid Culture*.

PATTI HAGAN has been the gardening columnist for *The Wall Street Journal* since 1986. Born in Honolulu, Hawaii, she has attempted to grow the flowers of her tropical birthplace — assisted by her cats Be-bop, Thelonious Monk, Ms. Mingus, Max Roach and Bird — in a Brooklyn brownstone the past 14 years.

LARRY HODGSON is editor of *House Plant Magazine* and *Fleurs, Plantes et Jardins*, a French-language gardening magazine. In his spare time he hosts TV and radio shows, writes a gardening column, does horticultural translation and leads garden tours abroad.

LAURA L. KRAMER is staff horticulturist at Ohio Indoor Gardening in Columbus.

TOVAH MARTIN has been a grower and the staff horticulturist at Logee's Greenhouses for 21 years. She is author of several books, including *The Essence of Paradise: Fragrant Plants for Indoor Gardens* (Little, Brown, 1991). She was Guest Editor of the Brooklyn Botanic Garden handbook *Greenhouses and Garden Rooms*.

ELVIN MCDONALD is the former Secretary of the American Horticultural Society and Director of Special Projects at the Brooklyn Botanic Garden. He has written more than 40 books on gardening, most recently *The New Houseplant: Bringing the Garden Indoors* (Macmillan, 1993).

C. C. POWELL served on the faculty at Ohio State from 1970 until 1992. He is president of Plant Health Advisory Services in Worthington, Ohio, which trains plant care professionals. He has written four books, including *The Healthy Indoor Plant* (co-authored with R. Rosetti).

Botanical artist and photographer **ROB PROCTOR** is a frequent contributor to *Herb Companion* magazine. He is the author of *Perennials* (1990), *Annuals* (1990), *Country Flowers* (1991), *The Indoor Potted Bulb* (1993) and *The Outdoor Potted Bulb* (1993), all published by Simon & Schuster

MARY ELLEN ROSS is co-owner of Merry Gardens in Camden, Maine, where she has grown 400 different varieties of geraniums. She helped found the International Geranium Society.

JOELLE STEELE writes monthly Question & Answer columns and feature articles for *Interior Landscape* and *Pro* magazines. She has published over 500 articles in addition to six audio tapes and several books for the interior and exterior landscape trades.

KATHERINE WHITESIDE is a freelance garden and travel writer. She was a consultant and writer for the eight-part PBS series and book *Gardens of the World*, which won an Award of Merit from the Garden Writers of America. She is also the author of *Antique Flowers* and *Classic Bulbs* (1991), both published by Random House-Villard Books.

LINDA YANG is author of *The City Gardener's Handbook: From Balcony to Backyard* (Random House, 1990) and a garden writer for *The New York Times*. She was Guest Editor for the Brooklyn Botanic Garden handbook, *Town and City Gardening*.

Introduction

BY TOVAH MARTIN

hy are houseplants so often approached with fear and trembling? Brave gardeners who don't blink an eye before tackling the trickiest gentian suddenly become weak-kneed when a begonia crosses their path. People who have gardened outside all their lives are rendered panic-stricken by a little bitty gesneriad. Why are houseplants so intimidating?

I think I have the answer. The fear of houseplants is due to lack of education. Houseplants are the last frontier. People hesitate because no one has shown them the way. Well, this handbook is meant to quell all those fears. In these pages, experts offer insights into every aspect of indoor gardening from seed sowing to fertilizing and repotting. They tell you how to set up a light garden if you lack window space, they tell you how to grow hydroponically if you don't want to fiddle with soil mixes. I suppose that a certain percentage of the population has avoided gardening indoors because they've only encountered the ho-hum houseplants sold in supermarkets. If you think houseplants are boring, this handbook should be a real eye opener. Some incredible indoor plants are available nowadays. Take plumerias, for example, or begonias, or pelargoniums, or gardenias — you'll meet them all herein. When you grow plants indoors, bright blossoms, profuse foliage and tantalizing scents can all be at your elbow regardless of the weather outside. If you have limited space, try something miniature. If you have nothing but a north-facing window, try a foliage plant. It might surprise you to learn that some orchids are easy enough to grow and coax into blossom in the average home. The experts tell all.

Finally, I've heard some folks whisper behind my back that a plant's place is in the garden, not on the windowsill. They claim that our ancestors didn't entertain living plants on their windowsills. Actually, they're absolutely correct — the colonists *couldn't* entertain live plants indoors. They didn't have sufficient light coming through their frugal windows, they didn't have enough heat from their open hearths. And they didn't have time to lug water from the pump for extraneous chores. In fact, the Puritans didn't have time for any leisure activities. They didn't grow ornamentals indoors or outside.

But things have changed. Architecture has evolved and today's homes are well endowed with glass. Modern heating systems keep the climate well above freezing both day and night. Meanwhile, modern humidifiers can put moisture back in the air when the furnace labors too long. Best of all, gardening is becoming a well-accepted leisure-time activity. Folks who have communed with nature all summer are having trouble spending a season or two deprived of its therapeutic and aesthetic qualities.

If you find yourself yearning for flora throughout the year, don't hesitate a moment longer. No more excuses. This handbook will come to your rescue.

Let There Be Light

A guide to bulbs, ballasts
and other artificial lighting basics

BY LAURA L. KRAMER

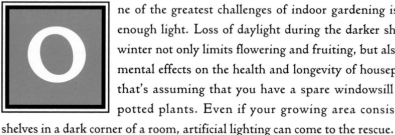

ne of the greatest challenges of indoor gardening is providing enough light. Loss of daylight during the darker short days of winter not only limits flowering and fruiting, but also has detrimental effects on the health and longevity of houseplants. And that's assuming that you have a spare windowsill or two for potted plants. Even if your growing area consists of some shelves in a dark corner of a room, artificial lighting can come to the rescue.

Light is essential for photosynthesis, the process whereby green plants use light energy to convert water and carbon dioxide to sugar and other carbohydrates. Plants utilize these products for food and to regulate physiological processes. Without ample light, photosynthesis and other biological processes are reduced or cease entirely.

Three properties of light are important to consider when choosing a primary or supplementary lighting system: quality, duration and intensity.

Quality refers to the color of the light emitted by a light source. The sun radiates light in all the colors of the rainbow. Plants need most of their light from red and blue areas of the color spectrum. Flowering plants need orange-red light in particular.

Duration, or photoperiodism, refers to the daily amount of light to which plants re exposed. Plants are classified as short-day, long-day or day-neutral, depending on the photoperiod that they require. Most plants need 14 to 16 hours daily.

Intensity refers to the amount of light available in a given area. This is measured n footcandles (the light intensity of one candle at a distance of one foot). Of all the actors limiting photosynthesis, intensity is the most critical. Consider that outside on , sunny day, the light intensity is somewhere around 10,000 footcandles. The average ndoor light level, on the other hand, is 50 to 150 footcandles.

Many different types of artificial light are available for indoor gardening. If you hoose a light source that emits the full spectrum of light, your plants should thrive.

HIGH INTENSITY DISCHARGE (HID) LAMPS

High intensity discharge (HID) lamps are the most effective and brightest lights

Halide lamps provide the best spectrum of light for all stages of plant growth. They are also six times more energy efficient than incandescent bulbs and last a long time.

available. These bulbs create light by passing electricity through a sealed glass or ceramic tube. The two most common HID lamps are the halide and sodium types.

Halide lamps are the most popular source of white light available for indoor gardening, providing the best light spectrum for all stages of plant growth. Not only is the light emitted from halide lamps comfortable to work around, but plants also appear most aesthetically pleasing when viewed under white light. The bulbs produce light up to six times more efficiently than incandescent light sources. They also have a long life expectancy and are available in a wide range of wattages.

Sodium lamps are the brightest of the high intensity discharge lamps. They provide more light from the orange-red area of the light spectrum, the range that stimulates flowering in plants. Because the light from these bulbs has an orange-red cast, you may want to use them in an unfrequented area or in a greenhouse. Sodium bulbs are also available in a wide range of wattages and typically last longer than halide bulbs.

Halide bulbs are recommended for situations in which there is little or no natural light. Sodium lamps are best for supplementing natural light. A combination of a halide and a sodium bulb will not only increase light intensity but also provide a full spectrum of light enhanced in the red-orange range. Sodium conversion bulbs are available which can be interchanged with a halide bulb in a halide lighting system to boost flowering.

What wattage bulb do you need? This depends on the size of your growing area, the light needs of the plants you're growing and whether the artificial lighting will be the primary light source or a supplement to natural light. See "How Many Watts?"

HOW MANY WATTS?

Lamp Type	Wattage	Growth Area (sq. ft.)
HALIDE	175	9
	250	12
	400	25
	1,000	64
SODIUM	150	9
	250	12
	400	25
	1,000	64

The orange-red light of sodium lamps stimulates flowering.

for some general guidelines.

A light source will keep your plants productive only as long as the light intensity remains strong. It's a good idea to monitor light intensity periodically with an accurate light meter. When lamp intensity has decreased, replace the bulb. A good rule of thumb: both halide and sodium bulbs should be changed after 12 months of use.

BALLASTS AND REFLECTORS

Once you've chosen the kind of light source for a specific growing situation, it's time to consider the ballast, reflector and other components of the system. Be sure the lighting system passes Underwriters Laboratory (UL) standards. It should be recommended by UL as safe for use around water and in damp areas. It should also have a full-size junction box for wire connections, and 600-volt wiring from the lamp to the ballast.

The ballast (the power unit that regulates the flow of electricity) should be horizontally oriented. It will run 25 percent cooler and last longer than a vertically oriented ballast. A heavy-duty 14/3 grounded power cord is highly recommended for all systems. Most lighting systems are designed to run off standard household electrical currents.

Reflectors should be painted white to increase light efficiency. Plain, polished aluminum does not reflect evenly, creating hot spots in your growing area. A double parabola reflector design ensures that all the light from the lamp is directed toward the plants.

Previously, many kinds of artificial lights were available for indoor use. However, many of them have been proved unacceptable. Armed with the information above, you should be able to grow healthy houseplants even if you don't have an abundance of natural light. ▦

Holistic Health Care for Houseplants

How to enhance your plants' ability to take care of themselves

BY DR. C. C. POWELL

 aintaining resistance to infections and infestations is a basic life process of any living thing, be it a human being or a house-plant. The things we do as caretakers of plants will be success-ful if they enhance the plants' ability to take care of themselves. This is basically what holistic or integrated health management is all about.

THE PLANT HEALTH BALANCE

What is a healthy plant? Good health involves a balance. If all of the environmental elements that are influencing a plant remain within reasonable ranges, a plant can bal-ance its internal processes to satisfy its needs. It remains a healthy plant.

The basic environmental elements that promote houseplant health are: a crumbly soil, a balance of nutrients, proper soil pH, enough space for crown and roots, ample water, moderate temperatures, good light, pure air and freedom from pests and dis-eases. When one or more of these elements is out of kilter, the health of the plant is at risk. So the first order of business in keeping your houseplants healthy is to maintain the proper environment for each.

Stresses cause houseplant problems. When confronted with an unhealthy plant, your first job should be to identify chronic environmental imbalances rather than merely treating the acute problem such as an infectious disease or insect pest. Put yourself in the plant's place. Investigate the soil or water situation, whether there's too much light, whether temperatures are too high or too low, whether the soil is compacted.

The yellowing leaves of this Japanese fatsia could be a sign of nutrient deficiency. It could also be the result of inadequate drainage.

Remember that environmental imbalances are apt to occur in combinations and may compound one another. For instance, soil dryness may not become stressful until temperatures climb. If dryness and high temperatures persist, spider mites may begin to develop.

ACUTE VS. CHRONIC STRESS

Plants, like humans, suffer from acute and chronic stresses. The former occur suddenly and cause damage quickly. Improper sprays, toxic chemicals poured onto soils, injuries during shipment, transit or handling at home, or day-to-day exposure to extremes of cold and heat are examples of acute conditions. Plants become unhealthy very quickly as a result of these problems. Chronic conditions, on the other hand, include nutritional imbalances, soil compaction, soil moisture problems, not enough light or improper soil pH, which can tie up nutrients and make them unavailable to the plant. Chronic conditions take time to affect a plant.

Dealing with chronic conditions sometimes is easier than remedying acute conditions. If you recognize signs of chronic problems immediately, you can gradually reverse the imbalance. On the other hand, there's little time to correct an acute problem

When faced with a plant stressed by insects or disease such as anthracnose, above, your first job should be to check for and correct environmental imbalances.

before disaster sets in. Usually, all you can do is learn from the experience and avoid repeating it. Chronic conditions eventually result in sick plants. The time it takes for the plant to become sick is called the period of plant decline. There are varying degrees of plant health, ranging from magnificently healthy to pathetically diseased. The longer a plant endures a stress-promoting condition, the more drastically it declines in health. The key is to recognize problems early and act quickly to reverse them.

NONINFECTIOUS AND INFECTIOUS PROBLEMS

Chronic environmental conditions often weaken a plant, leaving it susceptible to infectious agents. Managing these conditions can go a long way toward solving infectious as well as noninfectious problems. Of course, this is not always the case. Some disease organisms (such as crown rot) or pests (such as mealy bugs) are so infectious that they will attack even reasonably healthy plants.

SOME COMMON INSECTS AND DISEASES OF INDOOR PLANTS

It's a good idea to become familiar with the most common houseplant pests. The serious ones are mites, mealy bugs and scale insects. All of these are relatively immobile; once they arrive on a plant, these pests and their immediate offspring tend to stay on it. Their numbers may increase or decrease from time to time, but the infestation remains. As plants are moved about, the pests ride along. Often they are on the underside of a leaf or some other place that makes them hard to find, or their numbers may be so low that they go undetected. As long as you make sure the plant is not environmentally stressed, these pests cause no trouble. However, if environ- mental conditions change for the worse, the pests can rapidly multiply and spread to other plants.

The outside agent causing an infectious disease is called a plant pathogen. Many bac- teria, viruses, fungi and nematodes are

Diseases such as powdery mildew, above, are often caused by improper watering, too much or too little light or temperatures that are too high or too low.

plant pathogens. Most of them are microscopic and live on or in plant tissue as para- sites. Their activities on or in the plant cause abnormalities that lead to disease symp- toms. For instance, as a pathogen "robs" leaf cells of nutrients, it may also deposit enzymes or toxic waste products into the surrounding tissue. These substances may pro- duce yellowing, malformation or death of plant cells and tissues. The destruction of one part of the plant can cause problems elsewhere. Root rot causes wilt and yellowing of shoots, for example, because rotted roots cannot take up water and essential nutrients.

Keep in mind that the pathogen and the disease are not the same thing. Diseases don't spread from plant to plant — *pathogens* do. Fungicides can't control diseases, they control or kill the fungus causing the disease. You will have a better appreciation of manag- ing infectious diseases if you remember that it is the pathogen and not the symptom that you are trying to inhibit, eradicate or otherwise control. The most common infectious dis- eases of indoor plants are powdery mildews, leaf spots and root rots.

TEN TIPS

Holistic health management begins with plant selection and continues with proper care that will ensure your plants' environmental needs are being met. These two broad

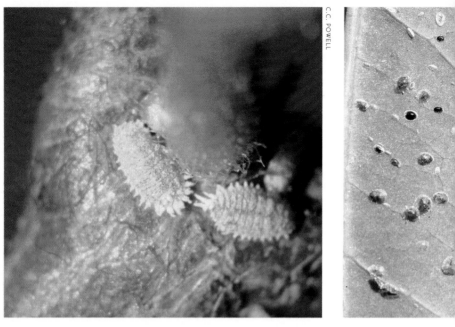

Insect pests from left to right: mealybugs, scale and red spider mites. The most effective pest-management strategy is prevention — closely examine plants you

strategies will prevent or control most pest and disease problems. If all else fails, you may need to discard a plant or else consider some stronger medicine. However, pesti‑ cides should be a last resort— they may eliminate the pest for the time being but do nothing to remedy the underlying environmental stresses that made the plant suscep‑ tible to the problem in the first place.

The following ten tips are designed to help keep your houseplants healthy.

1 Select plant species that are not overly prone to pests and diseases.

2 Be fussy about where you buy new plants. Some growers are more rigorous than others in their efforts to prevent and control pests. Many plant pests originate at the nursery or greenhouse. The most effective pest‑management strategy is prevention — buy only pest‑free plants.

3 Closely examine new plants. If possible, keep them quarantined for two to three weeks before introducing them to previously adopted houseplants.

4 Make sure that pests aren't brought in from outside by you or anyone else who comes into contact with outdoor plants. Many mites and insects are specially adapted to attaching themselves to clothing or skin.

5 Always work with clean hands and clean equipment. Periodically change, clean or disinfect all your gardening tools. Mites and insect pests are commonly spread

are considering buying. Purchase only pest-free plants. Select plant species or cultivars that are not overly prone to pests and diseases.

through contaminated equipment. Dusters, for example, can be fumigated in a box or bag with mothballs.

6 When watering, avoid touching plants with water breakers or hose extensions whenever possible. Avoid splashing water from plant to plant.

7 Isolate moderately and heavily infested plants. Dispose of them or treat them in quarantine. Sanitize all nearby surfaces after infested plants have been removed. Prune infested branches. Keep the plants quarantined for one month after the last treatment. Even then, inspect them carefully for hidden infestations and don't forget to check the roots.

8 Improve vigor of plants by improving root health: if the soil is compacted, loosen it up and add a bit of fresh soil, or repot if necessary. Increase the amount of light provided for the plant.

9 Increase humidity; avoid hot, dry areas. Lower fertilizer rates. Keep infested plants moderately moist at all times.

10 If you use pesticides, read and follow labels closely. If the name of the plant is not on the label, then it is probably inadvisable to use that product on your plant. Hose off as many of the pests as possible before spraying. Several applications of pesticide will probably be needed to control the problem.

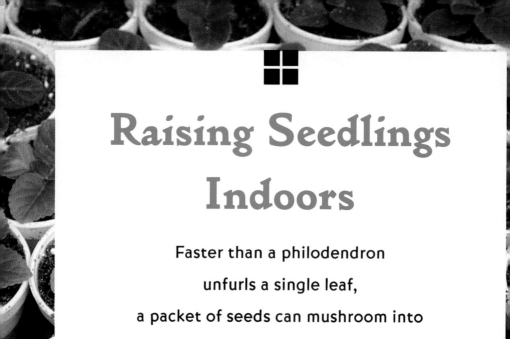

Raising Seedlings Indoors

Faster than a philodendron
unfurls a single leaf,
a packet of seeds can mushroom into
a flat of bushy transplants.
The joys of rearing baby plants

BY RITA BUCHANAN

ouseplants, for all their charms, aren't very dynamic. They don't *do* much. By contrast, seedlings change and grow from day to day. First a tiny sprout peeks above the soil and spreads its flap-like cotyledons. Before long, the first true leaves develop, already displaying the characteristic shape and fragrance of the species. Roots poke out the bottom of the container, and soon it's time for repotting. Every time you look, there's something new to see. Faster than a philodendron unrolls a single leaf, a packet of seeds can mushroom into a flat of garden-ready transplants.

Raising seedlings is fun, and there are many good reasons to give it a try. By starting your own flowers and vegetables, you can get a headstart on the season, save money and try interesting varieties that you'd never find at a local garden center. If you don't have much space for a garden, you can start plants for windowboxes, hanging baskets or patio planters. You can even start your own houseplants. Many kinds grow readily from seed. Try gloxinias, gerbera daisies and geraniums for bright flowers; coleus and polka-dot plants for colorful foliage; eucalyptus or palms for a tropical effect.

Starting seeds indoors avoids such outdoor risks as heavy soil, cold nights, splashing rain, glaring sun, dry winds, hungry birds and errant dogs. You can virtually control the weather indoors, providing ideal conditions for tiny plants, and you can make their lives easy and safe. No doubt about it, starting plants indoors gets the highest yield from each packet of seeds.

PROVIDING IDEAL CONDITIONS

Providing sufficient light is very important. Even if there are no cloudy days where you live, day length is still short in late winter and early spring, when you most want to start seeds. The solution is to use fluorescent lights. Simple shop-light fixtures, available at any lumberyard, building-supply center or discount store for under $15, do the job nicely. Ordinary tubes are okay; you don't need special grow-lights for seedlings.

You'll need to support the lights somehow, and to adjust their position as the seedlings grow. Seed catalogs feature manufactured light stands that look very nice, but you can easily make your own from boards, plywood and a handful of nuts and bolts. Some gardeners hook chains from the ceiling to support lights over a table or bench; others simply balance the ends of the fixture on bricks or books.

A 24-hour timer that turns the lights on and off automatically is a worthwhile convenience. Seedlings grow fastest with about 18 hours of light daily, so you might set the lights to turn on at 6 a.m. and off at midnight.

As for temperature, most seedlings do fine if the air temperature is between 60 and 75° F in the daytime. Fluorescent lights don't give off much heat, so the temperature underneath them is about the same as the room temperature. However, it doesn't hurt to check regularly with a minimum/maximum recording thermometer, especially if the seedlings are in a room far from the thermostat.

Don't even think of using ordinary garden soil for starting seeds. It's too dense and heavy. Some gardeners swear by screened, finished compost, but professional horticulturists always use commercial seed-starting mixes made of finely ground peat moss and vermiculite. These mixes are sterile; that is, free of weed seeds and disease organisms. They're lightweight, even when wet, so they don't stress thin-walled plastic trays and flats. Both the peat moss and the vermiculite absorb and hold moisture readily, but extra water drains quickly through the large pore spaces. The fine, granular texture of the mix makes it possible to spread a very thin layer over newly sown seeds. It also facilitates teasing apart the roots during transplanting.

Seed mix is very dry when it comes out of the bag, and should be moistened before using. I put some in a plastic dishpan, add hot tap water and stir thoroughly, then wait several hours for the soil to absorb the water. When you use the soil, it should be moist but not so wet that you can mold it into lumps or squeeze out water.

SOWING AND GERMINATION

You can sow seeds in all kinds of containers ranging from recycled milk jugs and yogurt cups to wooden flats, soil blocks and styrofoam plug trays. Anything that's shallow and drains well will work. I use small plastic pots about two inches deep. One pot can hold up to a few dozen seedlings. Soon after germination, I transplant the seedlings into the separate cells of plastic six-packs. To save time, you might sow a few seeds directly into the six-pack cells, thinning them later.

The most important part of sowing is spacing the seeds far enough apart. Crowded seedlings grow tall and skinny with weak stems. Also, tightly jammed seedlings are hard to separate for transplanting. Unless the package states otherwise, assume that you'll have nearly 100 percent germination. Try to position the seeds on the soil surface at least four times as far apart as they are wide.

Seed germination is often affected by light. Only a few plants, including vincas and delphiniums, demand total darkness. Most tiny seeds, such as begonias, and many medium-sized seeds, including coleus and impatiens, germinate better if they're exposed to some light (ordinary daylight inside a house is sufficient). Check the seed packet or catalog for more information on particular species. If no light requirement is specified, just spread a shallow layer of soil mix — about the thickness of the seeds themselves — over the surface of the pot.

Watering after sowing helps settle the seeds into place. The safest method is to set the pots in a shallow tray of water, letting the water wick up into the soil until the surface looks dark and shiny. Then set the pot aside to drain. A faster but riskier method is to apply a gentle spray with a mister.

Keep the seeds evenly moist until they germinate. A single drying-out can be fatal. The easiest way to maintain constant moisture is to put the pots into a plastic shoebox or sweaterbox, or cover the seedling flat with a sheet of glass or plastic. Thus protected, seeds will stay moist for weeks without additional watering.

Some seeds prefer warm or cool conditions during germination.

RITA BUCHANAN

Providing enough light for seedlings is crucial. Days are short in late winter when you're most apt to start seeds. The solution is artificial light.

Again, check the packet or catalog for specific requirements. Most flowering annuals and tropical houseplants germinate best if the soil temperature is between 70 and 80° F; it doesn't matter if the air is cooler than that, as long as the soil is warm. You might have a suitably warm spot on a radiator or heat vent, or you can purchase electric soil-heating mats from garden centers. Look for one with a built-in thermostat.

Most commonly grown seeds germinate in less than a month, and many pop up in less than a week. Check each pot daily. If you spot any emerging shoots, remove the glass or plastic lid and take the pot off its heat source. Extra heat and humidity can weaken tiny seedlings. What they need now is bright light and circulating air.

You can sow seeds in any kind of container, as long as it has good drainage.

Starting in one corner, carefully prod the roots of tiny seedlings free using a pencil.

CARING FOR SEEDLINGS

Seedlings become "leggy" if they don't get enough light. As soon as they emerge, position seedlings within two to three inches of the light tubes. As they grow taller, keep adjusting the pots and lights so the bulbs are just two to six inches above the leaves. The stems will stretch and grow weak if they are too far from the lights.

Careful watering is a necessity for seedlings, especially at the early stages. Some pots will need watering every few days, others require drinks less than once a week — it all depends on the kind of plant, how many there are in the pot, and how big they are. Check each pot daily; if it feels lightweight and the soil surface is light colored, it's time to water. A good watering method is to fill a shallow bowl with tepid water and lower the pot in the bowl to absorb water from the bottom up. A few seconds dip will saturate the soil. Another way to provide water is with a layer of capillary matting, a puffy synthetic-fiber fabric. Cut a piece of matting to fit under the pots of seedlings. Thoroughly wetted, it can absorb enough water to keep moistening the soil for a week or more.

Bottom watering is good for the roots; they grow deeper and stronger if the soil is drier on top and moister beneath. Also, keeping the surface of the soil dry helps protect the stems from"damping off," a fungal disease that attacks the stem tissue right at the soil line, so that the seedlings flop over and die. To prevent the problem, sow the seeds far enough apart to allow air to circulate between the young plants.

RITA BUCHANAN

To give them growing room, transplant seedlings into a new container.
Plastic six-packs can be reused.

Set seedlings slightly deeper than they
were in the germination pot to keep
them from flopping over.

As soon as seedlings have two or more true leaves, they benefit from frequent
applications of diluted fertilizer. I use a soluble houseplant fertilizer such as 20-20-20
or 15-30-15 once a week, mixing about 1/4 tsp. per gallon of water. Manure tea, fish
emulsion or seaweed extract also work well. Whatever you use, regular feeding promotes steady, vigorous growth.

Pests can be a problem. You can kill pests with a light spray of pyrethrum, insecticidal soap or highly refined horticultural oil. But be careful — any of these remedies
can scorch the seedlings' leaves. Try dislodging the pests with a spray of plain water
before escalating to anything stronger.

TRANSPLANTING SEEDLINGS

A few weeks after germination, when the seedlings have grown two or more true leaves (cotyledons don't count), it's time to transplant. Freeing a seedling from its neighbors requires careful handling. Always grasp a seedling by a leaf, not its stem — it can survive injury to a leaf, but a snapped stem is fatal.

For tiny seedlings such as petunias or thyme, start at one edge of the seedling pot and try lifting them out one at a time, using a pencil to prod the roots free. For tomatoes, peppers, zinnias and other vigorous seedlings, you'll do less damage to the roots if you tip the pot and carefully slide the whole soil ball out onto your work surface, then untangle each plant from its neighbors.

It's tempting to pot up every single seedling that germinates, but consider the consequences. Plants take up space. How many of those plants do you really need or want? Could you give away the extras? Decide at the onset how many seedlings should be saved, then choose the sturdiest ones for transplanting and discard the rest. That's the hardest part of raising seedlings.

You can transplant seedlings into all sorts of containers. I prefer preformed plastic six-packs. They're inexpensive, easy to sterilize for reuse (wash them in hot soapy water with a dash of bleach) and compact enough to store from year to year. They fit securely into plastic flats that are convenient for bottom-watering and for transport. Best of all, even heavily rooted transplants slide out of the cells easily with minimal trauma.

Whatever type of container you use, its size should match the size of the plant and its rate of growth. Tiny or slow plants need small pots; more robust plants can go in larger pots. When in doubt, choose a smaller-size pot.

There are two methods of transplanting. If the root system is large, or the roots are thick and brittle, hold the plant with one hand, suspend the roots in the center of an empty pot, scoop in some soil with your other hand, fill the pot to the rim and gently tamp it down. If the root system is small, or the roots are thin and fibrous, fill the pot first with loose soil, make a hole in the middle with a pencil or your finger, drop the roots into the hole, then push back the soil and tamp it into place. Never coil the roots as you transplant a seedling. Once they start growing around in circles, they never branch out properly.

I usually set a seedling deeper than it was in the germination pot, placing the cotyledons just above the soil surface. Setting the seedlings deep helps hold them in an upright position, so they don't flop over. There are exceptions: seedlings of sweet peas, lilies, grasses and other plants whose cotyledons remain below the soil surface should be replanted at the same depth as they were before.

GROWING ON

After germination, it usually takes 4 to 12 weeks for seedlings to grow big enough to transplant into a garden bed, planter or adult-size pot. Their primary needs during this time are plenty of light, careful watering and regular feeding. Keep adjusting the lights so they are just a few inches above the leaves. Group like-sized seedlings together to facilitate your light adjustments and check seedlings daily for watering.

Many seedlings benefit from being "pinched back"— that is, pruning out the growing tip to encourage side shoots to develop. Short, bushy plants are always stronger and more attractive than tall, skinny ones. At the same time, pinch off any flower buds that appear. Young seedlings shouldn't be wasting energy on making flowers; that can wait until after their roots and shoots are well developed.

Seedlings that are destined for the garden need time to adjust from the protected environment indoors to the real world outdoors. Allow several days for

Expose young plants to the outdoors gradually over several days before planting them in the garden.

the transition, a process called hardening off. The idea is to expose them gradually to hotter and colder temperatures, bright sun, drying winds and overhead watering. At first, set them out for only an hour or so in the morning or afternoon. Then leave them out all day, and finally leave them out day and night.

Even seedlings of houseplants such as geraniums may need time to adjust when they graduate from the lightstand to the windowsill. A sunny windowsill can get hot enough to wilt tender young plants, so it's a good idea to move them back and forth between lights and window for a few days. Of course, you could keep growing them under the lights indefinitely. But then you'd have to get more lights so you could raise more seedlings again someday.

Hydroponics & Hydroculture

A beginner's guide

BY JOELLE STEELE

o some of us, growing a plant without good old-fashioned "dirt" seems unnatural. We're so accustomed to seeing plants growing in soil that we assume they cannot grow properly without it. But plants do not require soil. In fact, plants grown in water alone (hydroculture) or in hydroponic systems (containers or units filled with water and such non-soil media as crushed rock or vermiculite) are often healthier than their soil-grown counterparts.

Hydroponics offers many benefits to gardeners. The sterile medium eliminates soil-borne pests and diseases as well as weeds, drastically reducing the need for toxic chemical controls. Lack of humidity is no longer a concern as the water supply provides atmospheric moisture.

Hydroponic gardening takes the guesswork out of watering and fertilization. Exact amounts of nutrients are given at specific intervals, and the plants use them as needed. Nothing is leached out of the root system, the roots do not grow as extensively in water as in soil and the plants make at least 20 percent more crown growth. They also take up less room and can be grown in individual pots and containers of whatever size, shape or configuration the available space dictates.

For beginners, basic hydroculture or water culture is an inexpensive introduction to this gardening method. One or two plants (of the same or different species) are displayed in containers filled with water and nutrient solutions. More advanced hydroponic systems may contain supportive materials such as charcoal and gravel.

CONTAINERS

For true water culture, almost any heavyweight, clear glass container of any shape or configuration may be used. For plants that require more support than water alone can provide, a layer of crushed rock in the bottom of the container will give the roots a foothold. Charcoal from your aquarium supplier can be used and has the added advantage of deterring the growth of algae, a harmless but unsightly green growth that sometimes covers the inside of the glass container, particularly if it is in a warm, sunny window.

Containers and any support media must be thoroughly sterilized before you introduce plants and water. Scrubbing with hot soapy water should do the trick. If you decide to grow a mature plant in water rather than rooting a cutting, you must also remove all traces of soil from the plant. Then place it into the container and slowly pour the water around the roots until part of the stem is underwater. If the leaves get wet in the process, be sure to blot them dry with a soft cotton towel.

WATER QUALITY

Because the purity of the water is important, it must be replaced at least once every four weeks. If algae form between changes, the container must be scrubbed out and all traces of the algae must be removed before the water is replaced. To help cut down on algae, reduce the amount of fertilizer you use. And, whenever the water level drops between monthly changings, add a little more water.

Water pH is also important. To measure the pH of the water, you will need a pH testing kit consisting of nitrazine paper strips. Check the water weekly. A pH reading between 6 and 7 is ideal. When the pH is not within these limits, the plant may not be able to use the available nutrients. If the water is too alkaline, (over 7), neutralize it by adding drops of vinegar or grains of aspirin, retesting after each drop or grain until the proper level is reached. Though it is not common, water that is too acidic (under 6) can be neutralized by adding bicarbonate of soda.

Chlorinated water affects pH levels, so let the water stand for 48 hours until this chemical dissipates before filling your containers. Never use artificially softened water. And if you decide to use a hydroponic system that collects drained-off water and nutrient solution, it should be reused only for a short period of time — three to four days at most.

NUTRITION

With hydroponic systems, almost any plant food can be used as long as it is water soluble. In addition, the manufacturer's package should state that it is a "complete fertilizer" specifically formulated for the types of plants you are growing. Reduce the amount recommended by about one third for use in hydroponic and hydroculture systems. The only time to fertilize is each time the water is changed. Fertilizers specifically formulated for hydroculture are available.

GROOMING

Plants grown in hydroponic systems do not require a lot of care, but they do get dusty and should be cleaned regularly so their pores do not become clogged. Remove any dead leaves from the plant or the surface of the media. Those dead leaves can decay and "pollute" your otherwise sterile system.

DIFFERENT METHODS

A variety of hydroculture and hydroponic methods are readily available in this country:
Continuous Flow Method involves three containers arranged at different levels

Hydroponic systems range from the simple to the high-tech. This relatively elaborate set-up has a built-in timer and pump.

with the highest containing nutrient solution with a tube leading to the middle container where the plant is located. Another piece of tubing runs from the bottom of the middle container to the lowest container. As the top container empties, it is refilled from the bottom one, recycling the water and nutrients. This is a workable system but may not be practical as it also requires aerating the solution with oxygen.

Gericke Method uses waterproof troughs topped by a wire grid with a mixture of peat and hay (or sawdust). The plants are stabilized in the media so their roots grow through the grid and into the nutrient solution below with a space for oxygen left between the grid and the liquid.

Other methods use traditional pots filled with substances other than soil.

Sand Culture consists of a pot filled with sand and water. But the sand usually becomes waterlogged unless it's mixed with gravel for improved drainage.

Aggregate Culture employs gravel, perlite, vermiculite and wood chips. Gravel or vermiculite is used in combination with sand for water retention, and the amount of sand used is determined by the frequency of watering. The less often you want to water, the more sand you use. This method requires some experimentation to discover the right combination of materials.

Flower Pot Hydroponic System relies on a variety of watering methods. Those systems in which water is passed through a growing medium and into a drainage reservoir are called "active" and those that rely on wicks or sub-irrigation are termed "passive." Automated sub-irrigation or wicks operate by means of capillary action to draw moisture to the root system from a reservoir. The gravity feed method consists of a bucket reservoir that feeds nutrients directly to the aggregate via a hose. The "slop method" has a pump that floods the surface of the medium with water, which seeps into the root system and exits through a drain into a container from which water and nutrient solution can be reused for a short time.

The simplest system is a plant growing in water.

It takes some experimentation to determine which system you want to use. Budget is certainly one consideration, as are available space and the quantity and kinds of plants you want to grow.

Hybridizing Cane Begonias

True fanatics can never get enough of their favorite plant
family. When you run out of plants to buy, hybridize.
A beginner's guide to crossing plants

BY WALTER DWORKIN

nce you're smitten with a specific plant family, you can never
get enough of it. These were exact sentiments when I fell for
cane (also known as angel wing) begonias. Cane begonias are
ravishing plants, with a wide range of different foliage shapes,
colors and sizes as well as beautiful pendulous flower clusters.

Even after I collected virtually every plant in circulation, I
still craved more. One thing leads to another, and I started to research the parental
backgrounds of these plants. In no time I was obsessed with creating my own hybrids.

A hybrid is the result of crossing two plants of different varieties, species or genera. The first lesson to learn before attempting hybridiziation is that begonias have
both female (seed parent) and male (pollen parent) flowers. Once you choose the
parents for your cross (hybrid), you must take certain precautions.

VIVE LA DIFFÉRANCE

Let's begin by exploring the characteristics of the male blossom. The male bloom is easily recognized because, unlike the female, it has no ovary compartment behind its tepals

(petals). The pollen is stored in pollen sacks of the anthers of the male blossom. In many instances, although pollen is present, it's not always visible to the naked eye.

When you decide to make your cross, choose a day that is dry with low humidity. (If it's a wet or humid day, the pollen will not transfer to the female flower.) Likewise, avoid making crosses early in the morning if you live in areas where there is heavy morning dew. Newly opened male blossoms are not mature enough to release pollen. The best males are mature, with fully opened tepals, and preferably ripe pollen exhibiting a darker shade of yellow. One good rule of thumb is to use male flowers that have fallen off the plant because their pollen sacks have definitely matured. Pollen can also be stored in the refrigerator or frozen for use at a later date.

Now that we are all experts on pollen, let's examine the role of the female blossom in hybridizing. The female flowers generally appear in clusters after the males have opened. They are generally larger than the males due to the triple-segmented ovary compartment located behind their tepals. Once mature, the female will begin to open its tepals to receive pollen. I begin to pollinate the female flower as soon as it opens and continue for the next couple of days. Early pollination is my only insurance against alien pollen (spread by bees, other insects or the wind) gaining entry.

TAKING PRECAUTIONS

To pollinate the female blossom, simply take the male blossom and gently rub its pollen sacks into the female's stigma. Be careful not to damage the female's reproductive parts. Then tag the female bloom and carefully document in a diary the date of the cross and the parentage, always listing the female parent first and the male second.

STEVE BUCHANAN

Transferring pollen

If the cross is successful and fertilization has occurred, the female will close its tepals and no longer be receptive to pollen. You will also notice discoloration of the female's stigma, shedding of the tepals and swelling of the ovary compartment. Once fertilization has occurred, you must wait at least five weeks to two months (praying all the while that your seed pod does not drop off). During this time, do everything in your power to protect the seed pod from damage by wind, rain, hoses and well-meaning plant-grooming friends. Once the pod has turned brown and its stem has shriveled to a threadlike state, it's time to harvest and place it in a labeled envelope until planting time.

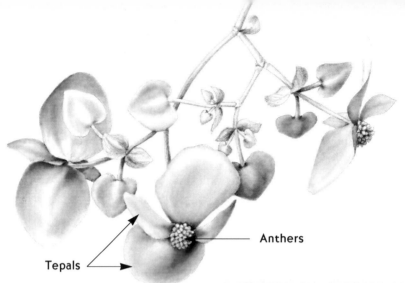

Tepals

Anthers

Above and right:
male flowers of the
honeysuckle begonia.

Seed pods that have been aged and dried properly can be turned upside down and the seed contents will come pouring out as from a salt shaker. If the seed doesn't spill out naturally, you can break the pod and sift the seed. Your harvested seed will be very minute, resembling pepper. If you lift and slant the paper in which your seed is resting, you will notice that the seed will start to roll — viable begonia seed is round.

AS YE SOW...

Sow your seed in a well-drained, sterile, soilless planting medium. The medium should be moist, but not soaking wet. Gently sprinkle seed evenly on top of the planting medium (begonia seed should not be buried). Next, spray the surface with a fine mist and wrap pot and all in a clear plastic bag. Keep your newly potted seed warm and covered in plastic to hasten germination. Most of the seed will germinate within 13 days; however, many seeds will sprout in as early as eight days, while others may take as long as two months. Once your seed has germinated, supply as much light as possible; good light will ensure compact, strong growth.

Tepals

Stigma

Ovary

Above: female flowers. In the photo, left, a female flower cluster is on the left and a male cluster is on the right.

During their developmental stages, two or three months, your seedlings will have a built-in immunity to mildew. Alas, this little blessing will be short-lived and you must examine the flat on a regular basis to check for signs of this killer disease. To keep your seedlings healthy, avoid overcrowded conditions and provide good air circulation. Better yet, when choosing parents for hybridizing, avoid those that are prone to mildew.

As the months pass by you'll feel like a proud parent watching your little treasures mature and exhibit a variety of beautiful colors, spots, stripes and leaf shapes. You'll find yourself on the telephone boasting that your hybrids are the greatest thing since sliced bread. I suggest that you refrain from making such telephone calls for about 24 months while your seedlings undergo some drastic changes. Today's pick of the litter could become tomorrow's dog.

The lot of the hybridizer is a mixed bag of rewards and disappointments, but in my experience the joy of success outweighs the heartbreaks. Every hybridizer rejoices when that special seedling inherits the best characteristics of both its parents, dazzling the world with its beauty.

Bulbs Indoors

The perfect solution for houseplant hedonists
who want lots of pleasure for relatively little work

BY KATHERINE WHITESIDE

eople have placed flowers in their houses for eons, but the idea of growing plants inside is a relatively recent notion, one that the ever-industrious Victorians elevated to yet another edifying art. The plants they started with were bulbs, "a few squat ugly bulbs that worked magic when planted," to quote *Once Upon a Windowsill*, a lively history of indoor gardening. After all, Victorian houses were cold, dark and often filled with coal smoke, so it was most fortuitous that bulbs — just about the most fool-proof bloomers around — were the first plants to undergo parlor cultivation.

Today, many busy, globe-trotting householders claim that they no longer have time for houseplants. And yet, there is nothing simpler than the annual pot of "forced" winter-blooming bulbs. Cheery crocuses, tulips or daffodils are the traditional choices for chasing away the cold-weather doldrums, but there are also many other accommodating candidates. Some of the most exotic-sounding and beautiful tender bulbs are truly indefatigable bloomers. And like all bulbs, they possess the most accommodating characteristic of slipping into a dormant period during which they need absolutely no attention at all. Bulbs are perfect for houseplant hedonists who want lots of pleasure for relatively little work.

Tete-a-tete' daffodils mingle with striped squill, *Puschkinia scilloides*, in a rustic aggregate container indoors.

WHAT IS A BULB?

Hortus Third, the Big Brown Bible of North American gardeners, decrees that, "When defined as a horticultural class, bulbs are ornamental, partial-season, mostly simple-stemmed plants arising from bulbs, corms, tubers or thickened rhizomes." Thus, the mighty *Chasmanthe* that charges upward from a small corm is just as much a bulb as the familiar tulip. Likewise, the stately calla lily that arises from a thickened rhizome and the tiny tubers of *Oxalis versicolor* that unfurl dainty peppermint parasols fall into the catch-all category of bulbs.

GROWING HARDY BULBS INDOORS

The term "hardy" is so loose that it rattles. Plants considered to be hardy in the British Isles often won't survive two minutes during a New England winter. For our purposes here, we will relegate bulbous plants that thrive outdoors after a normally cold winter (temperatures often below freezing) to the hardy bulb group. This would include most tulips, narcissi, crocuses, alliums, fritillaries, muscaris and so on. Many of these plants are the most familiar bulbs for indoor use. But be forewarned that not *all* hardy bulbs work well inside. Professionals recommend that beginners try hardy bulbs that are relatively early-season bloomers with stems on the shortish side, and most gardening catalogs mention whether or not a bulb is suitable for forcing. However, once you get the hang of the simple routines required for flowering, feel free to try forcing any hardy bulb that catches your fancy.

For ordinary garden use, hardy bulbs are usually planted outdoors in autumn because they require a long cool period of very active root growth. A strong root structure must be developed before the top leaves and flowers can grow. Thus, it also makes sense to provide this root-growing period when you grow hardy bulbs indoors. Commercial growers have devised very exact time and temperature schedules to produce pots of flowering bulbs at precise marketing times. Household growers can relax a bit and enjoy the process.

In autumn, pot bulbs such as early tulips, narcissi, hyacinths, muscaris and crocuses in new, store-bought bulb potting mixture. Alternatively, you can make your own potting concoction by mixing the following in equal parts: good garden soil, leaf mold, well-rotted manure and sharp sand. The best looking containers are clay pots (with good drainage holes), which should be soaked in water for several hours before being filled with soil. The bulbs may be planted closely but should not touch one another. The top of the bulb should be even with the rim of the pot and, with tulips, the flat side of the bulb should face the outside of the pot. Don't mix different bulbs in the same po

– they rarely bloom simultaneously.

Once you've made up all your pots, water well and promise faithfully that you won't let these bulbs dry out during their rooting time. Next, take all the pots to your dark, unheated basement, garage, attic or outdoor cold frame — in other words, stash them in a spot that will not reach over 48° F for at least the next two months, but one where the pots will not freeze and thaw. A word of caution: tulips and crocuses are especially yummy to animals who will eagerly dig up all your best efforts. Liberally sprinkling red pepper has proven a wildly successful deterrent.

Parrot tulips are a medium height and can be forced to bloom indoors.

If you potted your bulbs in early October, start checking their progress in early December. The best way to ascertain adequate root growth is to carefully remove the soil from around one of the bulbs and peek underneath. If you see roots, re-cover the bulb and leave this pot in place to settle down after your excavations. Choose another pot, or two or four, to bring inside for the next stage of forcing, keeping in mind that if you bring in new pots every two weeks, you'll have successive waves of indoor flowers for a long period of time. On the other hand, if your careful digging revealed little or no root growth, leave all the pots in the cold and check again in another two weeks.

Following their cold, dark rooting period, the ideal position for forcing hardy bulbs is in a window that gets as much light as possible but remains cool. Remember that hardy bulbs bloom outside when it's still sweater weather — you will have the best and most long-lasting flowers if you can find a sunny window that stays around (preferably under) 55° F. Once you've brought the pots inside, they will usually sprout leaves and flower in about three to four weeks. At flowering time, you may place your beautiful plants wherever you please, but keep in mind that cooler is better. A position of honor on the mantle — with a cheery fire glowing underneath — will soon reduce your weeks of waiting to a one-night burst of glory.

Most forceable bulbs can be purchased from dealers who will give more specific directions for each type. Some of the easiest and prettiest hardy bulbs for indoor win-

ter forcing are: crocus, chionodoxa, muscari, *Fritillaria meleagris*, lily-of-the-valley
Scilla siberica, snowdrop, hyacinth, tulip, narcissus and *Iris reticulata*.

Although there are exceptions, it's generally difficult to force the same pot of
hardy bulbs year after year. Bulbous plants require a ripening period for many, often
unlovely, weeks to build up their underground storage tanks for next year's growth
spurt. Months and months of floppy, elongated and yellowing foliage are really not
worth the few dollars you'll keep by attempting to save your bulbs for another season.
After you've enjoyed your winter bulbs, just throw them away.

TENDER BULBS INDOORS

To many inexperienced indoor gardeners, the thought of growing tender bulbs seems
pure folly — a difficult and expensive venture doomed to fail. However, if the truth be
known, tender bulbs are actually easier to cultivate than hardy ones because they don't
need a dark, cool preliminary rooting period. They grow roots and tops at the same
time. Also, for the soft-hearted or penny-pinching, many tender bulbs can be saved
year after year — they actually flower better after several years' cultivation.

Three South African plants — tall, swordlike *Chasmanthe aethiopica*, the graceful white calla (*Zantedeschia aethiopica*) and the dainty *Melasphaerula ramosa* —
are so alike in their cultural needs that they can easily be mentioned in the same
breath. Since they all come from the southern hemisphere, their natural flowering
time is our winter. Thus we don't really force these bulbs, we just give them a hos-
pitable position in which to carry on their normal blooming season. Corms and rhizomes of these plants are available in mid-summer and should be planted immediately. Chasmanthes and callas need large pots, melasphaerulas prefer a small pot. Potting soil is the same as the medium recommended for hardy bulbs, but these long-lasting bulbs should be buried at least one inch deep, leaving room in the pot for later top-
dressings of compost. Do not water the pots at all at this time and, if possible, place
them outdoors where they can bake in the sun but remain completely dry. Sometime
in autumn, check your pots — green shoots should begin appearing. Bring the pots
indoors, place them in a sunny window and give them water — southern hemisphere
spring has started.

Water is important now. Chasmanthes and melasphaerulas need frequent watering, but should never get soggy. Although it's seldom recommended by modern bulb
books, best results with callas come when the entire pot is kept standing in a bowl
filled with water. (The Victorians recognized the aquatic nature of the calla and grew
it in water with great success.) Bulb expert Martyn Rix recommends high potash
feeds such as Tomorite, but watering with fish emulsion and top dressing with com-

ost also promotes strong, healthy lants.

After several months of producing eautiful leaves, your South African ets will begin to bloom. *Melasphaeru- a* swings wiry wands with up to ten mall, irislike white flowers per stem. *Chasmanthe* shoots up tall stems of yel- ow or red hooded "flowers" (technically nflorescences), sometimes sending tems as high as four feet. The calla nrolls "flower" after "flower" resem- ling white vellum. Your southern hemi- phere flower show will last for weeks.

After flowering is finally over, the oliage will begin to decline. Allow the eaves to ripen (these never seem to each the unbearably unsightly stage), hen cut everything off at soil level. You

Tender bulbs like glads are even easier to grow indoors than hardy bulbs.

re now back to the stage where you began, except, after a season's growth, the soil hould be compacted enough so you can place the pots on their side in some out-of- he-way place in your garden. Let them bake dry all summer, and in autumn, begin hecking for the sprouts that signal a new cycle of growth.

There are many tender bulbs suitable for indoor growing. Some additional ones to try are: *Agapanthus, Amaryllis, Crinum, Gladiolus, Clivia, Oxalis, Nerine, Lachenalia, Ixia, Moraea* and *Gloxinia.* All these bulbs are readily available from catalogs and specific instructions for each plant are available from suppliers.

Keep in mind that indoor bulb growing is not limited to the ways and means mentioned above. Water-forcing is a pleasurable and simple method and is especially suitable for certain narcissi, crocuses and hyacinths. Basic instructions are: place peb- bles one inch deep in a shallow bowl; position the bulbs on top and add a few pebbles around the sides of the bulbs to steady them; add water to the bottom of the bulbs; and place them in a sunny window. Keep the water topped up, but do not allow the bulbs to rot. Leaves and flowers will soon sprout.

Of course, there are also bulbous plants that may be grown indoors during the other three seasons. However, to many, the joy of growing bulbs indoors comes from the pleasure of easily having out-of-season flowers to cheer up our wintery houses.

Little Wonders for Small Spaces

Horticulture in miniature
is a concept rife with possibilities.
How to grow plants so small you may need a magnifying
glass to fully appreciate their beauty

BY ELVIN MCDONALD

ardeners who grow houseplants have an unusual opportunity to admire at close range plants so small that a magnifying glass may be needed to fully appreciate their beauty. Miniatures save space, making it possible to grow many different varieties in a given area. Some miniatures are ideally suited to growing in individual small pots, from the size of a thimble up to an inch or two, while others may succeed better if set in a larger container. The pitfall is that tiny pots can dry out before you've scarcely turned your back. To apply water, purists use miniature watering cans, and they perform their pruning chores with delicate manicure scissors rather than the loppers wielded in the big garden outdoors.

Horticulture in miniature is a concept rife with possibilities. Instead of a row of sill specimens in soldierlike procession, try working them into a trayscape garden either casual or formal in design, inspired by Eastern or Western notions about gardens. The study of bonsai is an ideal way to learn about all aspects of miniature horticulture. The individual plant specimens can be variously trained as trees, shrubs,

Rebecca Tyson Northen, the doyenne of orchids, inspects the flowers of a miniature specimen.

vines or ground covers. Some are suited to becoming miniature tree-form standards, espaliers or topiaries.

The plants below are old standbys that have given me wondrous houseplant experiences for 30 years; others are new to my collection.

Acalypha godseffiana 'Heterophylla' is native to New Guinea, a close relative of the famed "chenille plant," and a nonstop producer of tiny, tufted "chenilles" But the main attraction is the narrow skeleton leaves colored bronze, copper, cream, green and yellow on thin vertical stems that top out at 12 inches in height. This tropical will defoliate if subjected to temperatures below 40° F. Provide sun or partial sun.

Bougainvillea 'Pink Pixie' is a fraction of the size of regular bougainvilleas. Shell-pink bracts and pink flowers appear all along the stems between the very small leaves. It grows to about 12 inches in height. Needs full sun.

Ceropegia woodii, the rosary vine, is ideal for a six-inch wreath set upright in a three-inch clay pot. It can also be used in grander designs — as an arbor or pergola in a miniature landscape, for example. Provide full sun or partial shade.

Cyrtanthus species and hybrids look like miniature hippeastrums. They come in luscious pastels, bloom over an extended period and can be readily grown in a sunny apartment. The permanent collection of living plants at the Brooklyn Botanic Garden has some of the loveliest cyrtanthuses in cultivation.

Gardenia jasminoides 'Prostrata Variegata' is a perfect replica in miniature of a regular gardenia with little leaves with creamy white margins. Appropriately small flowers open intermittently all year and smell divinely of gardenia.

Hippeastrum, amaryllis, often earns its keep by being large. However, collectors crave the smaller species. The late Marcia Clint Wilson of Texas was an early champion of smaller, evergreen, repeat-blooming amaryllis. She gave me a bright pink blooming amaryllis with a green star in the throat and a citron yellow miniature that I have cherished for nearly 20 years, long enough to lose the name tags. Marcia's collection now resides with Steve Lowe, horticulturist at the zoo in San Antonio, who has continued her work. The commercially available 'Scarlet Baby' from the Netherlands is a good plant with which to start your collection.

Hoya lanceolata ssp. *bella* 'Variegata' is a summer-blooming form of the dwarf bush wax flower with short, trailing stems hidden beneath thick, waxy, lime-green leaves, each with a distinct dark green margin. It can cascade from a small basket or be

Angel wing begonia 'Tiny Gem', opposite page. Diminutive plants in tiny pots like this dry out quickly. Purists apply water with miniature watering cans. At left is *Crassula lycopodioides pseudolycopodioides*.

coaxed up and around a six- to eight-inch circle to form a living wreath.

Impatiens 'Hawaiian Pink' and 'Hawaiian Scarlet' resemble the common bedding impatiens, but in miniature. This three-inch impatiens smothered with bloom could come in handy as an edger or ground cover in a tiny garden or flower show exhibit.

Nematanthus wettsteinii, the miniature goldfish plant, is an extra-small version of a gesneriad that has small, waxy leaves and orange pouch flowers in profusion. It can be accommodated in a three-inch hanging basket with stems cascading down six inches, or the pliable stems can be trained into a four- or five-inch wreath.

Porphyrocoma pohliana is a miniature member of the acanthus family from South America. A rooted cutting in a two-inch-square pot will grow hardly more than four inches tall in a year. The persistent foliage is silver with burgundy underneath, while each stem is topped by a long-lasting ruby bract holding purplish flowers resembling sage blooms. Provide half sun to half shade.

Rosa, the rose genus, includes an array of micro-miniatures and minis, bushes, trailers and climbers. They look adorable in a sunny, airy window, or in a fluorescent-light garden (you'll need at least four 40-watt tubes in a reflector six to ten inches above the tops of the rose plants with an oscillating fan to keep the air moving). Try

training a micro-miniature into a diminutive tree-form standard six inches tall in a three inch pot. Train a dozen or more as an alleé in a very small formal garden indoors.

Miniature African violets or *Saintpaulia* have made it big time on the strength of being cute and nearly self-reliant. In the system developed by the Holtkamp family, each flowering violet has its own clear plastic reservoir filled with enough water and nutrients to keep it going for at least a couple of weeks. Optimara Violet Food, NPK 14-12-14, is the product designed to make this system work, along with average room temperatures and light bright enough to read by. There are many other miniatures, including micro-minis and trailers. Like their large-size ancestors, they have a tendency to produce clusters of small leaves at the base of the plant ("suckers"), and they fail to flower if the soil becomes too dry between waterings.

Serissa foetida 'Floro Pleno', the snow rose, is a gardenia relative that has tiny leaves like boxwood and double white flowers resembling tiny gardenias or minute white roses. It is highly trainable as a bonsai or tree-form standard and does well in a bright window or under fluorescent light. There are several cultivars, some with variegated leaves, others with single or pinkish flowers.

Sinningia 'Tinkerbells' was bred by the late Elena Jordan in her lower east side New York City apartment where she grew plants in available light with no artificial

Crassula deceptrix is on the opposite page. *Leptospermum scoparium*, New Zealand tea, in full flower is at left. Miniature plants can be trained as tree-form standards, shrubs, vines or ground covers.

supplements. This could explain in part why 'Tinkerbells' grows so easily when given half a chance. No other miniature is quite like 'Tinkerbells', whose small olive-green leaves are reddish on the reverse, on wiry stems to about six inches tall. The flower is tubular, small and delicate and rosy purple with a dark-spotted white throat. Elena gave me a rooted cutting about 20 years ago that has now formed a tuber the size of a medium potato — huge for a miniature sinningia. It grows in a six-inch plastic bulb-pan that came outfitted with a clear plastic dome. In bright light but no direct sun, or directly beneath the tubes of a fluorescent light garden, 'Tinkerbells' blooms about nine months of the year. It will grow more vigorously if dried off and kept at moderate temperatures for a semi-dormant period of three months. 'Cherry Chips' and 'Zelda' are more recent hybrids, bred in the Brooklyn basement of the late Marty Mines under fluorescent lights. They stay in a compact rosette and produce relatively large, notably brightly colored flowers.

There are easily enough tiny or miniscule orchids to keep any collector busy for at least a lifetime, not to mention miniature pelargoniums (geraniums), begonias (such as the miniature trailing 'Tiny Gem') and succulents (such as aloe, *Crassula lycopodioides pseudolycopodioides* and *C. deceptrix*) There are dorstenias galore (*D. mecca*, for example), and tiny creeping peperomias. And don't forget the highly trainable dwarf pomegranate, *Punica granatum nana*.

The Indoor Herb Garden

When winter arrives, you don't have to
retreat to your living room and sulk.
You don't have to pay the exhorbitant prices
fetched by herbs at the specialty market.
A cold season survival guide

BY ROB PROCTOR

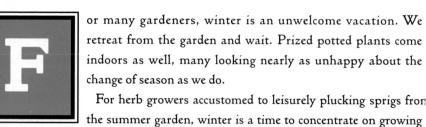

or many gardeners, winter is an unwelcome vacation. We retreat from the garden and wait. Prized potted plants come indoors as well, many looking nearly as unhappy about the change of season as we do.

For herb growers accustomed to leisurely plucking sprigs from the summer garden, winter is a time to concentrate on growing favorites indoors. Some herbs continue to supply fresh leaves for stews and salads, while others can be coaxed to bloom or display ornamental foliage.

In the eyes of many gardeners, the most important herbs for window culture are those for the cook. We balk at the exorbitant prices fetched by herbs at the specialty market (if we can find them at all). The solution: grow them indoors.

Many cooks rely heavily on rosemary, thyme, chives and bay. These perennial or shrubby herbs are easily accommodated on most bright windowsills across the coun-

A kitchen herb garden includes, clockwise from top left: oregano, chives, sage, mint and lemon balm. Drying herbs hang above.

try, and will perform even better in a greenhouse. Other potted herbs that present no great challenge include sage, winter savory and a wide variety of mints. Container culture is even preferable for many of the mints to keep their rambling roots from conquering the entire garden.

The addition of citrus flavors to tea, pastries and salads is especially pleasant in winter. Lemon grass and lemon verbena mimic their namesake well. The former is relatively easy to keep going in a sunny window, where its leaves can be snipped, but the latter is a challenge. It often goes completely dormant, leaving a twiggy skeleton that only revives when the days become longer in spring.

Annual herbs, such as parsley, basil and nasturtiums, can be brought indoors as winter approaches. Use them while starting others. Often, cutting an herb back severely while continuing to fertilize will force new growth. Other annuals, including coriander, fennel, chervil and dill, can be started from seed and will be ready for use in just a month or so. Thinned seedlings are equally useful for garnish.

Ornamentals and aromatics for the window or fluorescent light garden include society garlic (*Tulbaghia violacea* 'Silver Queen'), which displays handsome, variegated leaves, although it must be positioned in a well-ventilated room. *Tulbaghia fra-*

These herbal topiaries spend the summer outside and the winter indoors.

Nasturtiums can come inside as winter approaches.

grans has broader foliage and large clusters of lavender-pink or white blossoms that smell delightfully like hyacinths. Several tender species of lavender embellish the window herb collection, among them *Lavandula dentata, L. lanata, L.* x *latifolia* and *L. stoechas*.

Try holding over salvias from the autumn garden. *Salvia elegans*, aptly named pineapple sage, is prized for its fruitily aromatic leaves, brilliant red flowers and adaptability indoors. Other appropriate indoor salvias include the bright-flowered Texas scarlet sage (*S. coccinea*) and *S. gesneriiflora*, whose orange flowers are set off by chocolate-brown stems. At the opposite end of the color spectrum are *S. caerulea* (formerly *S.*

A handsome container garden mixes herbs, succulents and houseplants.

Culinary sage grows easily in pots indoors.

guaranitica), with deep blue flowers, and *S. involucrata* 'Bethellii', with rosebud‑like blossoms much too pretty to let freeze. Many of the tropical and subtropi‑cal sages don't get around to flowering until winter, so they make a dramatic statement on the sun porch. A number of these salvias attain dramatic proportions as well — five feet in height or more — so provide a suitably large display area.

While common sage, *S. officinalis*, is hardy across much of the country, it has several fancy‑leaved forms that require winter protection. Some have leaves with cream and pink margins, while others are bronze or mottled mint green. These culti‑vars make striking pot plants or add to mixed plantings in containers. They can also

JUDY WHITE

Chives can grow on a sunny windowsill.

Peppermint-scented geranium is another good candidate for indoors.

be trained into simple standards. Other herbs also make easy-care topiary — rosemary and scented geraniums, for instance. Very light winter pruning keeps them in shape and provides leaves for cooking as well as sachets.

Bringing potted herbs indoors can strain them. They often sulk when faced with the lower light levels, compounded by the shorter days of winter. Many perennial herbs need a period of rest and will make their intention clear, dropping leaves and ceasing active growth. Low humidity levels indoors, caused by central heating, may result in leaf-tip browning and curling. It can be a dismal sight. There's no use pumping them full of fertilizer or drowning them with kindness. It will only hasten their

Parsley grows well indoors. Here, curly and Italian parsleys grow together.

JUDY WHITE

Basil, which is tender and loves warm weather, is suitable for indoor culture.

emise. The best way to cope is to give potted herbs a very bright position supplemented by artificial light. Reduce watering by 50 percent or more until new growth begins.

Spider mites, white flies and aphids are commonly encountered pests for indoor herbs. Spider mites thrive when humidity levels drop. Grouping plants together (the buddy system") increases humidity around the plants, as does adding gravel to pot saucers. Excess water fills the spaces between the gravel and raises humidity levels as it evaporates. A good sudsy bath in the kitchen sink helps to keep white fly and aphid populations down.

Geraniums

Geraniums for topiary,
geraniums with scented leaves,
geraniums with black blooms edged with gold...
there's a whole world of geraniums
beyond the local garden center

BY MARY ELLEN ROSS

NANCY BROWN

or blooming plants in a sunny window, geraniums are hard to beat. Of course, I'm talking about the plants that are known botanically as pelargoniums, introduced from South Africa to Europe early in the 17th century by Dutch traders. Botanists originally believed these to be closely related to the hardy geraniums already growing wild in the northern hemisphere. So, in 1753, the Swedish botanist Linnaeus described 25 species of these plants from South

Regal geraniums, such as *P.* x *domesticum* 'Josephine', above, produce showy, azalealike blooms. They set bud only when night temperatures are below 60° F.

Africa under the genus *Geranium* in his *Species Plantarum*. Thirty five years later, L'Heritier, a French botanist, proved that they had been classified incorrectly and he coined the name *Pelargonium*. The public was unimpressed. To this day, we still say "geranium" when we mean "pelargonium."

From about 300 known species of pelargoniums, thousands of cultivars have evolved. To make it easier to identify the various types, different groupings were devised. Highlights from the groups follow.

Pelargonium x *hortorum*, the horseshoe or popular florist geraniums, resulted from a cross of *P. inquinans*, a single-flowered red species, with *P. zonale*, a species bearing single red blooms as well as a dark horseshoelike ring marking each leaf. From this cross, the Standard and French types were developed. Standards are tall growing and

HOW TO GROW GERANIUMS

LIGHT

In winter, geraniums need all the sun they can get. From December to February, the sun's rays are not strong enough to promote buds on some varieties. From May to October, they benefit from light shade during midday. Geraniums grow best at night temperatures of 50 to 60° F. They will survive down to 32° F and above 80° F, but must be treated as semi-dormant and kept dry at either extreme.

SOIL

Most any type of soil mix is suitable for geraniums. They prefer a pH of 6.5 to 7, so additional lime is beneficial. I use equal parts loam, peat and perlite in my mix with a complete fertilizer such as 4-12-4 or a slow-release type like Magamp, which I add at the rate of 1/2 cup per bushel of mix. I also add one cup of dolomite lime.

WATER

Too little or too much water causes the leaves to yellow. Allow plants to approach dryness, then water thoroughly. During winter when light levels are low, geraniums should be even dryer between waterings.

DISEASES

Diseases often pose more of a problem than insects for geraniums. Black leg and virus are the most common afflictions. Black leg is a fungus that attacks bruised or cut ends and rots the stem either from the roots useful in making topiary. The French type are more compact and became the parent of our modern day bedding and dwarf geraniums.

Many commercial growers produce their annual crop of Zonale geraniums from seed. There is a wide variety to choose from, such as the dwarf "Gremlin Series"and the vari-colored "Orbit Series." Earliest to bloom is the "Pinto Series." The tetraploids in the "Tetra Series" have extra large flower heads.

---

upwards or from the tip downwards. In either case, cut off the diseased part and treat the cut end with fungicide. Be sure to destroy all diseased parts to prevent the fungus from spreading to other plants.

Prevention of disease is paramount because there are no cures. Controlled watering and scrupulous sanitation — keeping dead and yellowing leaves and flowers picked off, using sterilized soil and using clean tools — can do much to prevent disease.

Some problems are difficult to detect. A plant may be infected with virus and still look healthy during its growing season. However, one sure symptom of virus is yellow or brownish spots on the young growth. When signs of virus are detected, it's best to discard or at least isolate the infected plant.

Thick, leafy growth appearing at the base of a plant is called leafy gall or fasciation. It does no great harm but should be removed because it competes with the roots for food. Little is currently known about the cause of this phenomenon. It is best not to take cuttings from an affected plant.

During long periods of rainy weather, leaves turn yellow rapidly, making conditions ideal for the growth of a gray fungus called botrytis. This may not be a problem in the home where humidity levels are usually low. Keeping yellow leaves and dead flowers picked off will help.

Because geraniums are fast growing, an occasional cutting back of the growing tip will help keep them low and bushy. On most varieties, it will take three to four months before blooming continues. Tall plants can be pruned back to two or three nodes from the base of the plant and new growth will quickly develop. For winter blooms, cut plants back in August. For Memorial Day blooms, pinch in February.

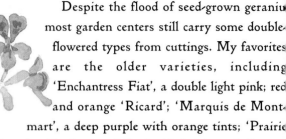

Despite the flood of seed-grown geraniu[m]s most garden centers still carry some double-flowered types from cuttings. My favorites are the older varieties, including 'Enchantress Fiat', a double light pink; red and orange 'Ricard'; 'Marquis de Mont-mart', a deep purple with orange tints; 'Prairie Dawn', with glowing, fully double bright pink flowers; and 'Modesty', with an abundance of large, snowy white blooms.

In the rosebud group, 'Appleblossom Rosebud' is hard to resist. It bears beautiful, white- and pink-edged double blooms in tight clusters. Each floret looks like a tiny rosebud. 'Red Rosebud', 'Pink Rosebud' and

P. quercifolium 'Fair Ellen'

P. x *domesticum* 'Roger's Delight'. Regal geraniums such as this will bloom for a long time on a sunny windowsill.

Magenta Rosebud' all have similar clusters of rosette-haped blooms.

Then there is the cactus or poinsettia type of Zonale with curled and twisted petals, so named because it resembles cacti or poinsettias. 'Cherry Poinsettia' is my choice for red, Hilda Conn' is a personal favorite in salmon and 'Noel' is the best white.

NANCY BROWN

FANCY-LEAVED ZONALE GERANIUMS

Grown primarily for their colored foliage, fancy-leaved geraniums are beautiful even without blooms. Fancy-leaved geraniums also have their groupings — the silver-leaved types, gold- and bronze-leaved hybrids and the tricolored types displaying combinations of white, silver, red and bronze. 'Skies of Italy' is the strongest tricolor, with maple-shaped leaves painted with bands of yellow, bronze and red. Its small, single, orange blooms are insignificant compared to the brilliant foliage. 'Mrs. Henry Cox', introduced in 1879, is not as bushy as 'Skies of Italy', but the leaf color — brilliant tones of yellow, red and pink — is more intense. 'Miss Burdett Coutts' is even more difficult to grow. Its colors are more pastel silvers pinks and bronzes.

P. fragans 'Nutmeg'

In the silver-leaved group, the popular 'Wilhelm Languth' is most robust, but a little tall growing. It blooms freely with medium-sized, double, cherry-red flowers. Mrs. Parker' is lower growing but not as strong. It has double light-pink blooms. These are only a few of the more than 50 fancy-leaved geraniums available today.

THE MINIATURE GERANIUMS

Perhaps the ultimate in Zonale geraniums are the miniature and dwarf types. In the mid-1940s, there were only two that could be considered truly dwarf or miniature. They were 'Black Vesuvius', which originated in England about 1890, and 'Mme Fournier', introduced in France a few years later. Credit for the modern day dwarf and miniature geraniums goes to two California hybridizers, Ernest Rober and Holmes Miller. Rober used 'Black Vesuvius' and 'Mme Fournier' to produce his famous "Seven Dwarfs," while Miller independently employed the same parents to create 'Pixie', a dark-leaved dwarf with single salmon flowers. Other hybridizers soon joined in. Today there are several hundred named varieties with such fairytale names as 'Goblin', 'Red Riding Hood', 'Pigmy' and, of course, 'Snow White' and 'Bashful', 'Doc', 'Dopey', 'Grumpy', 'Happy', 'Sleepy' and 'Sneezy'.

How do the dwarf and miniature geranium differ from the regular Zonales? They all have very small leaves, short internodes and bushy growth. They seldom grow taller than 12 inches, and the real miniatures do not exceed six inches. However, their stature is affected by sunlight, fertilizer and other factors.

ODD AND RARE GERANIUMS

The odd and rare group is comprised of species of interest mainly to collectors, but a few are distinctive and very attractive. *P. violarium*, a semi-trailing type, has lance-shaped gray leaves and blooms much like those of a pansy. The flowers of *P. echinatum*, the sweetheart geranium, are single white with a red heart-

P. 'Skelley's Pride'

shaped center. They are borne on long stems above steel gray leaves and thorny branches. *P. glaucifolium*, the black-flowered geranium, bears scented, dark maroon flowers edged with gold. On the other hand, *P. fulgidum*, the celandine-leaved storksbill, has woolly, gray-green, musky scented leaves and dark garnet-red blooms.

THE REGAL GERANIUMS

The Regal or Martha Washington geraniums (*P.* x *domesticum*) produce spectacular azalealike blooms, but they have their drawbacks and are primarily used as a holiday plant for Easter and Mother's Day. They set bud only when night temperatures are below 60° F; consequently, unless you have a greenhouse or cool plant room, it's best to buy them from your florist after the buds are set. Then you can enjoy a long period of blooms in a sunny window until hot weather sets in. Cuttings root best in the fall when plants should be cut back, repotted and grown in a cool, 45 to 50° F greenhouse. Keep them on the dry side until February, when they can be fertilized and watered more frequently. Unlike the Zonale geraniums, they need more water during their budding and blooming period.

White fly and aphids can be a major problem. However, they can be controlled if you watch your plants closely, use a soap spray when the insects first appear, then pick off the leaves that show white fly nymphs on the underside.

As with the other groups, there are many regals to choose from. A few of my favorites are 'Flower Basket', with salmon pink flowers, the earliest to bloom even during hot weather; 'Josephine', which grows rather tall but is a constant bloomer, with pink and white flowers even in the heat of summer; and 'Black Lace', popular for the novelty of its all-black flower. There are also pansy-flow-ered and miniature regal geraniums. 'Mme Layal', introduced in France in 1870, is still the best pansy-faced flower, with small blooms of royal purple and white. 'Spring Park', in the miniature regal group, blooms all summer with white, pink-eyed small blooms and fra-grant, bright green leaves.

THE SCENTED-LEAVED GERANIUMS

SOURCES

SHADY HILL
821 Walnut St.
Batavia, IL 60510
(708) 879-5665
Catalog: $2

LOGEE'S GREENHOUSES
141 North St.
Danielson, CT 06239
(203) 774-8038
Catalog: $3
(refundable with first order)

MERRY GARDENS
P. O. Box 595, Mechanic St.
Camden, ME 04843
(207) 236-9064
Catalog: $2

The scented-leaved geraniums are grown primarily for their attractive, fragrant foliage. Like the regal geraniums, most scenteds bud only when temperatures are below 60° F. While pretty, the blooms are mostly small, usually in shades of pink or lavender. 'Clorinda' and 'Roger's Delight' have more spectacular blooms like those of the regal geraniums. They have many of the same cultural needs as the regals although they are not as susceptible to white fly.

Enjoy their scents and use the leaves in cakes, teas, punch, butters, salads and salad dressings. Rose, lemon, lime, nutmeg, and peppermint are the types used in cooking. Popular scents are rose, strawberry, orange and lemon.

IVY-LEAVED GERANIUMS

The ivy geraniums (*P. peltatum*) are trailing, vining types with glossy leaves resem-bling ivy. Although they bloom at all seasons, they don't make good houseplants because they need cool temperatures, strong light and fresh air.

Rarities for the Indoor Garden

Unknown to most gardeners just ten years ago, frangipanis, bougainvilleas and other tropical species have become the hot houseplants of the 90s

BY RICHARD & MARY HELEN EGGENBERGER

hen we're selecting tropical flowering houseplants, we look for plants with the following traits: compactness, ease of bloom, long flowering season, eye-catching shapes and colors, low maintenance and, whenever possible, fragrance. With these virtues in mind, we've composed a list of our favorite choices.

PLUMERIAS

Unknown to most gardeners ten to 15 years ago, plumerias have become some of the most prized tropicals of the 90s. Many of the new hybrids bear immense clusters of flowers with individual blooms often five to six inches across! The array of colors is astounding as is the spectrum of scents, ranging from lemon to rose, jasmine, spice and even coconut.

Because plumerias are native only to southern Mexico, northern South America and the Caribbean, they were once considered impossible to grow in non-tropical areas. However, through research and experimentation, enthusiasts have found that plumerias can easily thrive throughout the U.S. outdoors during hot weather; in

Top: *Plumeria* 'Dean Conklin', left, and *P.* 'Loretta', right
Bottom: *P. obtusa* 'Singapore', left, and *P.* 'Tomlinson', right

unrooms, greenhouses, under lights or stored in a dormant state during winter.

Plumerias are often called frangipanis, a common name that has been traced to two derivations — the first in honor of the Italian nobleman, Frangipani, who invented the intoxicating perfume with the plumeria fragrance that became the favorite of Catherine de Medici. The name may also stem from French settlers in the Caribbean who called the plant "frangipanier," or coagulated milk, alluding to the heavy latex that flows from a cut in the tree. In addition, plumeria is often called the lei flower in Hawaii, its adopted home.

Top: *Bougainvillea* 'Helen Johnson', left, and *B.* 'California Gold', right
Bottom: *Hibiscus* 'All Aglow', left, and *H.* 'Tylene', right

Tip cuttings (do not use stem cuttings) of plumeria root easily if the latex at the base of the cutting is allowed to dry out. Place cuttings in coarse perlite and provide bright light but no direct sun. Keep them somewhat on the dry side. The best season for taking cuttings is spring to mid-summer. Cuttings of hybrids should flower the first year after rooting.

Although a few extraordinary dwarf forms exist, most plumerias can be kept compact by fertilizing with a low nitrogen and high phosphorus fertilizer. Plumerias are heavy feeders and respond best to regular fertilizer applications during the rowing season. Plants are long lived and long blooming, often flowering for months t a time, usually from mid-spring through fall. They are sun- and heat-loving plants - the more, the better. A minimum of five hours a day is recommended for optimum bloom outdoors. Their moisture requirements are moderate to light, and they prefer a well-drained soil rich in organic matter.

BOUGAINVILLEAS

Bougainvilleas make excellent container specimens and can flower many times a year. Today, with new hybrids continually appearing, the selection of compact varieties suitable for house culture is excellent and includes a veritable palette of showy bract colors and leaf variegations.

Plenty of bright sun is a must for sturdy growth and to promote cascades of bloom so massive that they completely cover the vine. A minimum temperature of 50° F is also preferable during the blooming season. What's more, there is a secret to encouraging bougainvilleas to flower, which we learned during our years in India from the bougainvillea expert, Mr. B. A. Rama Rao of Madras: after plants are well established in their containers, gradually withhold water, just to the point of shock. Begin by giving water only on alternate days. After a week, water every third day. After another week, water only once a week for a week or two. Then hold back watering for ten to 14 days. The leaves will droop or even fall from their branches. Now you can begin a regular program of fertilizing and watering, encouraging the plants to burst into bloom. Although this seems like a drastic treatment, it replicates nature's conditions in their native Brazil, where plants go through long, dry spells followed by heavy rains. For best results, use a fertilizer formulated for bougainvilleas or one fairly high in nitrogen, only moderate in phosphorus and high in potassium with all the trace elements, especially magnesium, in abundance.

HIBISCUS

Few plants can rival hibiscus in their extraordinary range of colors and color combinations, flower shapes and sizes and ability to produce continuous bloom throughout the year. Hibiscus hybridizers have developed single and double flowers in shades of blue, brown, yellow, gold, orange, red, pink and every color in between, with some flowers exhibiting three or more colors in a single blossom. They have also bred compact plants, some bearing blossoms that last two to three days. Current emphasis is on creating blooms with good substance as well as clear color and exceptional keeping quality. In addition, some hybridizers are now turning their attention towards developing fragrant blooms by crossing the few fragrant species that exist in nature.

There are a few important cultural requirements you need to know in order to grow beautiful hibiscus. At the top of the list is fertilizer. Unlike so many tropical that flower best with ample amounts of phosphorus, hibiscus need *low* phosphoru and high potassium. They would perish if given the same fertilizer as plumerias! To much nitrogen will push growth at the expense of bloom.

Hibiscus are attacked by a number of pests, ranging from aphids to white fly t mealy bugs. We have found that insecticidal soaps, pyrethrins and diatomaceou earth are effective. An occasional brisk spray of plain cold water will wash off aphids One of our most successful and inexpensive controls is a simple formula tha immediately kills adult white flies: mix two tablespoons of household vinegar and tw tablespoons of household ammonia per gallon of water, spray the infested plants an watch the amazing results.

DWARF GINGERS

The dwarf gingers also offer a wide range of flower shapes, sizes and colors, and the are virtually insect and disease free. They often have fragrant leaves or blossoms and in some genera, beautifully marked and colored leaves as well. Among our favorite are:

GLOBBA WINITTII, dancing lady ginger — If we must choose a favorite dwar ginger, this is the one. The dancing lady is graceful in every sense of the word. From mid-summer through fall this lovely plant will be in constant bloom. First the long pendulous inflorescences unfurl. Next, the glowing lavender-pink bracts emerge followed by the delicate golden flowers that look like miniature ballerinas. Matur plants bear numerous inflorescences to six inches or more in length, emerging from compact, lush blue-green foliage. Plants may be increased by division in spring. Us plumeria fertilizer (see above) or any time-release fertilizer high in phosphorus *Globba winittii* prefers shade or filtered light and can be grown and brought to bloon in small containers. Few plants are as carefree as this gem.

KAEMPFERIA GALANGA — Another dwarf ginger of special merit, *Kaempferia galanga* has dark green, rounded leaves with prominent veins. The sparkling white violet-shaped flowers have a striking royal-purple spot on the lip. Plants of thi species rarely exceed six inches in height.

KAEMPFERIA ROTUNDA — Commonly called resurrection lily or tropica crocus, this is a rare form of peacock ginger, with striking markings of pale, silvery lavender on elongated leaves. Numerous lovely, purple-tinged white flowers with lila lips appear in the spring before the leaves emerge. The resurrection lily can b flowered in a six-inch pot year after year.

Top: *Globba winitti,* left, *and Kaempferia galanga,* right
Bottom: *Kaempferia rotunda,* left, and *Mandevilla sanderi* 'Red Riding Hood', right

SMALL FLOWERING VINES

There is a wealth of small flowering vines that can be grown in containers for the indoor garden, sunroom or greenhouse. Some of the loveliest bloomers are:

MANDEVILLAS — These modest vines produce masses of blooms and do best in warm, sunny conditions. You can use a water-soluble or time-release plumeria fertilizer (see above) or a fertilizer high in phosphorus with excellent results. Among the finest cultivars are *Mandevilla* x *amabilis* 'Alice du Pont', with very large, brilliant rose-pink flowers; *Mandevilla sanderi* 'Red Riding Hood', a compact plant that makes an excellent hanging

SOURCES

THE PLUMERIA PEOPLE
P.O. Box 820014
Houston, TX 77282-0014
Catalog, $2

LOGEE'S GREENHOUSES
55 North Street
Danielson, CT 06239
Catalog, $3

Passiflora 'Jeanette'

basket with glossy, bronzy green leaves and deep rich pink flowers; *Mandevilla sander* 'Rosea', a small vine with clear rose-pink flowers each with a yellow throat; *Mandevilla boliviensis*, which bears white, trumpet-shaped flowers with glowing yellow throats se dramatically against glossy, dark green leaves; and *Urechites lutea*, a close relative with bright yellow flowers set against glossy green leaves.

CLERODENDRUM – Both *Clerodendrum thomsoniae*, a modest climbe prized for its lovely red flowers set in puffy white calyces, and *Clerodendrum* speciosum with scarlet-red flowers set in magenta bracts, are long blooming and d best in morning sun with shade or filtered light in the afternoon.

JASMINES – It would be possible to go on and on about the marvelous jasmines, whic justly top the list of the world's most fragrant flowers. Our favorite, again among many, i the 'Belle of India', a modern cultivar of the sambac (or Arabian) jasmine. Similar to th popular *Jasminum sambac* 'Maid of Orleans', this variety bears fully double flowers wit numerous petals and a fragrance that will perfume an entire room. Dried blooms add a exotic flavor to tea. Plants bloom almost continuously from spring through fall.

PASSIFLORAS – Most passion flowers grow too rapidly to be considered for th indoor garden unless you have ample room. There are a few, however, that have mor compact habits with shorter internodes. Our particular favorite is *Passiflor* 'Jeanette', almost always in bloom from spring to fall and one of the easiest to flowe Blooms are approximately three inches across and a rich lavender-blue color with pin shading and a darker purple corona. Other hybrids are becoming available fro hybridizers around the world.

The African Violet Family

A little bit of rainforest for your living room

BY LARRY HODGSON

he African violet family, also known as the Gesneriad family, is composed of some 125 genera and over 200 species. That's not a lot as far as plant families are concerned, but gesneriads never-theless take up a proportionally large share of our indoor grow-ing space, and no wonder — they perform and bloom indoors over and over again.

The reason gesneriads do so well indoors is because the average interior is quite similar to their native habitat. Most gesneriads grow as understory plants in tropical forests. They're adapted to moderate light, periodic drying, varying humidity levels and warm tempera-tures the year round. These same condi-tions prevail in the average living room.

Gesneriads are generally divided into three groups, depending upon their storage organs (or lack of them): fibrous rooted, tuberous and rhizomatous.

FIBROUS-ROOTED GESNERIADS

This is actually a group formed by default: any gesneriad that doesn't bear tubers or rhizomes is called fibrous rooted. It is by

African violet (*Saintpaulia* species)

far the largest category, and it also contains the largest number of popular houseplants.

African violets (*Saintpaulia* spp.) are the most popular fibrous-rooted gesneriads. The wild species native to eastern Africa all look quite similar, typically with violet-shaped, five-lobed, blue flowers. In culture, through mutation and hybridization, they have become an extremely varied group of plants. Double and semi-double flowers are now common in shades from white to pink to red and pale blue to deep purple. There are even yellow- and green-flowered and multicolored African violets. They range in size from micro-miniatures scarcely larger than a quarter to plants that spread wider than a foot across. Most form low-growing rosettes, although there are also multi-stemmed trailers. Their foliage can be all green or variously marbled in white, pink or tan.

Next in popularity is the *Streptocarpus*, or Cape primrose, which bears long, tongue-shaped leaves directly from the roots, showing no visible stem. Most streptocarpus form rosettes but some species produce only a single leaf during their entire lives. The flowers are generally borne on slender stems high above the foliage. They are distinctly trumpet-shaped and come in all shades except yellow, orange and green. The closely related genus, *Streptocarpella*, bears flowers that are very similar but smaller than those of the streptocarpus. However, the leaves of the streptocarpellas are notably different: they are small, oblong and borne on branching stems.

Streptocarpus 'Ultra Nymph'

The genus *Episcia* is also well known for both its interesting foliage and showy flowers. The leaves are attractively marked in various metallic shades from green to white to purple to red — some even have leaves that are shocking pink. The tubular flowers are produced on short stalks and are often brightly colored, with brilliant orange-red the most common shade. Episcias have another striking characteristic: they produce creeping stolons (stems) with plantlets at their tips displayed to best advantage in a hanging pot. Plants in the genus *Alsobia* also have stolons, but they bear small green leaves and highly fringed white flowers.

The genus *Chirita* is becoming more popular. The best known species is *Chirita sinensis*, with thick, stiff leaves in a dense rosette. The leaves of most cultivars of this plant are marbled in silver, and the purple flowers are very similar to the blossoms of African violets.

EPIPHYTIC GESNERIADS

Many fibrous-rooted gesneriads have adapted to living not in the ground, but on tree trunks and branches. These types, called epiphytes, generally have smaller, thicker leaves and longer hanging or upright branches than their terrestrial cousins. They are well adapted to extreme conditions and prefer drier soil conditions than other gesneriads.

The genus *Aeschynanthus*, from Asia, is often called the lipstick plant because its brightly colored flowers poke out of tubelike calyces. The leaves generally have a waxy texture, and the narrow, tubular flowers are often bright red or orange. The genus *Columnea* is very similar in appearance but hails from the New World. Most aeschynanthuses bear their flowers in clusters at the ends of their stems during a brief season, whereas columnea species and hybrids produce flaring, yellow to red flowers along the leaf axils over a longer blooming period. Due to those flaring tubes, columneas have been nicknamed goldfish plants.

CHARLES MARDEN FITCH

Columnea 'Red Spur'

Although *Nematanthus* are closely related to columneas, they scarcely resemble them. Their small, often shiny leaves are borne on trailing stems. The small orange, yellow or red flowers are tubular with a large bulge at the base, giving them quite a curious look and earning them the equally intriguing nickname of guppy plant. Nematanthuses hail from South America.

Without flowers, plants in the genus *Codonanthe*, from South and Central America, look a lot like nematanthuses with small leaves on trailing stems. However, when they come into bloom, the small, flared, white flowers reveal their true identity. The two genera have been crossed with standard-sized plants, producing the hybrid genus x *Codonatanthus*, which has characteristics of both.

Some gesneriads form large, generally underground storage tubers, rather like woody potatoes. Most tuberous species go completely dormant after flowering, losing their foliage entirely. Just take your cue from the plant and stop watering until it sprout again several months later.

The florist gloxinia, *Sinningia speciosa*, is by far the best-known tuberous gesneriad. But this sin-ningia's bell-shaped flowers are hardly typical of the genus — in fact, the wild species bear trumpet-shaped flowers much like those of the streptocarpus. Florist gloxinia flowers tend to be beautifully spotted and can be just about any color except yellow, orange or green. Double-flowered varieties are also available.

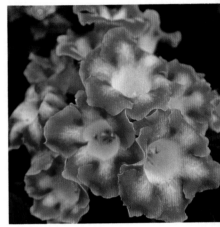

Sinningia speciosa, florist's gloxinia

Numerous other sinningia species and hybrids are widely available. *S. cardinalis* bears cardinal red, nar-rowly tubular flowers over hairy, apple green leaves and upright stems. The sim-ilar *S. canescens* (formerly *S. leucotricha*) is so totally covered in white hair that its foliage appears quite silvery. Even the flowers are fuzzy! *S. eumorph* bears rosettes of large bronze leaves and slipper-shaped flowers, generally whit or pink.

Very different is the tiny *S. pusilla*, scarcely larger than a nickel, with equal tiny lavender, trumpet-shaped blooms. Its need for high humidity makes it a goo choice for terrarium culture. *S. pusilla* and the related "micro-miniature" species, *S. concinna*, have been crossed to give a wide range of hybrids called miniature sin-ningias. Most are four to six inches in diameter and have trumpet-shaped flowers in wide range of colors. Miniature sinningias rarely go dormant; new stems are produce before the older rosettes have died. The same plant will remain in bloom most of th year.

The only other tuberous genus of horticultural importance is *Nautilocaly*. These are extremely beautiful plants, often with deep reddish or hairy, quilted, silve marked leaves. The flowers are generally hidden among the leaves. The most popul member of the genus is *N. lynchii*, with dark, shiny purple leaves.

RHIZOMATOUS GESNERIADS

Gesneriads in this group produce scaly rhizomes at the end of one growing season that die back once growth has begun the following spring. Each plant produces many rhizomes, so multiplication is a snap. Another propagation method is to scrape off the scales at the beginning of the growing season and sow them like seeds. Each will produce a plant.

Although rhizomatous gesneriads can and should be allowed to dry out entirely during their dormant season, they need ample water during the growing season or they will slip into premature dormancy or perish entirely.

The best known rhizomatous gesneriad is *Achimenes*. Widely available in bulb catalogs, it is strictly a summer grower, sprouting in spring and dying back the next fall. It is used indoors and out, often in hanging baskets. The wide-faced trumpet flowers are large in relation to the size of the plant and are available in literally every color of the rainbow.

Achimenes longiflora

Plants in the genus *Kohleria* have thick stems and large hairy leaves, often attractively marbled. The flowers are trumpet shaped with striking contrasting spots on a yellow, pink, red or green background. *Kohleria* flowers are borne at leaf axils, a trait that is the major difference between them and the similar genus *Smithiantha*, whose flowers are borne in clusters at the tip of the plant. Many smithianthas have velvety maroon or deep red leaves which really don't have their match elsewhere in the plant kingdom. Flower colors tend to be various shades of yellow with contrasting red spots and marbling.

EASY TO GROW

Gesneriads grow best in bright light with some morning sun. They're particularly floriferous under fluorescent lights. Lack of light often results in healthy foliage but few or no flowers.

Saintpaulia 'Dolly'

Although gesneriads prefer humidity, especially when in bloom, they will tolerate dry indoor air. Average indoor temperatures are fine, as are most light potting mixes. For maximum bloom, feed your plants regularly with flowering plant fertilizer. Gesneriads generally prefer their potting mix to be kept slightly moist. During the dormancy periods, hold back the water from tuberous and rhizomatous types. Epiphytic gesneriads should dry out slightly between waterings.

Propagation is easy. You can take stem cuttings, but most gesneriads (especially those with thick leaves) will also readily produce plantlets from leaf cuttings. Most gesneriads are also especially easy to grow from seed, often blooming within a year after sowing. The seeds are extremely tiny and should not be covered with potting mix as light is necessary for germination.

Easy to grow, easy to bloom, gesneriads are also, for the most part, very easy to find. In addition to local nurseries, there are hundreds of mail-order specialists devoted to African violets and other gesneriads. You'll find their ads in the publications of the various gesneriad societies listed below:

African Violet Society of America
P. O. Box 1401
Beaumont, TX 77704

African Violet Society of Canada
1573 Arbordale Ave
Victoria, British Columbia V8N 5J

American Gloxinia and Gesneriad Society
c/o The Horticultural Society of New York
128 West 58th St. New York, NY 10019

Gesneriad Society International
1109 Putnam Blvd
Wallingford, PA 19086

Saintpaulia International
1650 Cherry Hill Road South
State College, PA 16803-3214

The Leaves Have It

Palms for Victorian parlors,

cacti for Santa Fe-style interiors,

clipped topiaries for classical decor — there's a foliage

plant to suit every taste

BY LINDA YANG

hen green thumbs are blue with winter cold, the indoor sill is the garden location of choice. Take the scene at George and Virginie Elbert's upper west side New York City apartment, which is landscaped with over 500 houseplants — give or take a pot or two. Windowsill space has been extended by tiers of shelves and movable tables, and every cranny is covered with vegetation.

The Elberts' collection of tropical plants includes many that are appreciated more for their decorative leaves than for blooms, and their gardening fervor for these species approaches missionary zeal. "Foliage plants — as we call these kinds — are easy. Any-one can grow them and everyone should," in the words of Mr. Elbert. For, even dur-ing long, winter-darkened days, plants like asparagus fern, spathiphyllum, philoden-dron and sansevieria manage to thrive.

On the other hand, houseplants grown primarily for flowers demand more effort, attention and light. Where conditions are difficult, few of these do well after their first blooming. Some may even be discarded. "But foliage plants are permanent residents — like pets," according to Mrs. Elbert. "What I like most are the many different leaf shapes and variations of color — green on white, green on yellow, with pinks, reds, blotches and stripes."

FOLIAGE PLANTS FOR WINDOWSILLS

Plants that Tolerate Bright Reflected Light

ASPIDISTRA ELATIOR MINOR

ARDISIA CRENATA

CORDYLINE TERMINALIS 'Tricolor'

PEPEROMIA OBTUSIFOLIA

MARANTA LEUCONEURA

LEEA COCCINEA

Plants that Tolerate a Minimum of Three Hours of Sunlight Daily

ALOE VERA

CITRUS RETICULATA 'Dancy'

NOLINA RECURVATA

ALPINIA ZERUMBET 'Variegata'

ANANAS COMOSUS 'Variegatus'

KALANCHOE BEHARENSIS

Citrus reticulata 'Dancy'

GEORGE ELBERT

Plants that Do Best with a Minimum of Five Hours of Sun Daily

PORTULACARIA AFRA 'Variegata'

JACARANDA MIMOSIFOLIA

PACHYPODIUM LAMEREI

ROSMARINUS OFFICINALIS

ZAMIA FLORIDANA

Spathiphyllum 'Lynise'   *Aechmea fasciata*

The Elberts'dedication to indoor landscaping dates back to around 1960 when they first moved to a New York apartment. They have since helped found the Indoor Gardening Society, which now numbers over 2,000 members nationwide, and co-authored more than a dozen books.

In the past 30 years, the Elberts have witnessed indoor gardening trends, many of which, they suspect, were a function primarily of what commercial growers made available at the time. Asparagus ferns, grape ivy and philodendrons were in wide use in the 1960s. Designers found these plants were useful not only for softening severe architectural styles but for surviving long periods of poor growing conditions. In the 70s, the presence of shopping malls and atriums led to the introduction of large foliage species whose scale was suited to vast public spaces. It was not long before designers discovered that these tree-size weeping figs, cycads, palms, fiddleleaf figs and dracaenas were sufficiently versatile to serve in homes as free-standing sculptures. They could also be grouped together, creating living screens to divide up space. In the spare modernist vernacular, it was legitimate to use plants, not furniture, to fill the void.

Throughout the 80s and into the 90s, post-modernist trends have meant that a wider variety of architectural styles need to be satisfied, and growers now scramble to accommodate designers' visions. Aspidistras and palms seem cozily at home, for example, amidst Victorian trappings. Odd or spectacularly shaped cacti, bromeliads and euphorbias presently grace Memphis or Sante Fe style interiors. And formal clipped topiaries of rosemary or myrtle enhance classical decor.

But plants are living things. And unless the intention is to replace them regularly,

Dracaena tricolor

they must be chosen not only for their architectural contribution to a room, but for their ability to tolerate the environmental conditions within that room.

Beginners should start with plants that are easily grown and not be concerned that everyone may have them, Mr. Elbert advises. "A well-grown foliage plant can be a superb decoration for a troublesome spot. Why be a snob about commonly found plants?"

Those just starting might consider a spider lily, which has long, white striped foliage; or the variegated basket grass (*Oplismenus hirtellus* 'Variegatus'), whose dainty, pink-hued, striped leaves dance on top of pinkish stems; or possibly a dumb cane plant, whose bold, oval-shaped foliage is marbled with green and white. These plants withstand less than an hour or two of sun, are rarely bothered by pests or diseases and are most forgiving of neglect.

Also tolerant of less than ideal indoor landscapes is the lady palm (*Rhapis excelsa*) which has dark green, ribbed leaves whose ends appear to have been fringed with pinking shears; and *Alocasia* 'Fantasy', whose 15 inch-long, arrow-shaped leaves have wavy edges. For them, minimal sun or only bright light will suffice.

Of particular interest, too, are foliage plants that are fragrant. For double service — decoration and culinary use — there is sweet bay (*Laurus nobilis*), whose dark green, leathery-looking leaves tolerate as little as two hours of sun daily. Somewhat more demanding of sunlight is the Jamaican allspice tree (*Pimenta dioica*), whose oblong, fragrant foliage is also useful in stews. And then there are the many scented geraniums that can be added to potpourri or jellies. Among the Elberts' favorite scented geraniums are 'Dr. Livingstone', with finely cut foliage that emits a perfume redolent of lemon and roses, and the sweetly scented apple geranium, which has rounded, softer textured leaves.

Although foliage plants from the tropics are now taken for granted, they have served as indoor decoration only since the middle of the 19th century, according to Tovah Martin, author of *Once Upon a Windowsill* (Timber Press, 1988), a history of indoor plants. "Until the Victorian era, plants lived outdoors and we lived indoors — the cultivation of houseplants is a relatively recent event," writes Ms. Martin. "The early Colonists did bring in a few of their practical garden herbs. But tropical plants didn't arrive in North America until the advent of the 19th century plant explorers and the invention of the Wardian case, the glass enclosure that permitted long distance transport of plants."

Large foliage plants are relatively inexpensive, but there's an advantage to starting with smaller specimens. If you buy them when they're young, they'll adjust more easily to your conditions.

Acclimatizing large plants that have recently left the ideal conditions of a commercial greenhouse may occasionally be a trial for both plant and plant owner. Lost leaves and drooping branches are classic symptoms of "plant shock." Some species have particular difficulty adjusting. The Ming aralia, for example, doesn't like being moved at all and shows its distress by dropping its parsleylike foliage immediately. The weeping fig can also be temperamental in this way. "Give them time to get over their sulks," Mr. Elbert says, "If you can just resist overwatering and feeding them, they'll soon recover and grow new leaves."

SOURCES

GLASSHOUSE WORKS GREENHOUSES
Church Street
P. O. Box 97
Stewart, OH 45778
Catalog $1.50

KARTUZ GREENHOUSES
1408 Sunset Drive
Vista, CA 92083
Catalog $2

LAURAY OF SALISBURY
432 Undermountain Rd.
Salisbury, CT 06068
Catalog $2

LOGEE'S GREENHOUSES
141 North St.
Danielson, CT 06239
Catalog $3

RHAPIS GARDENS
Box 287
Gregory, TX 78359
Catalog $2

Adapted from an article that first appeared in *The New York Times*.

For Happy Gardenias

Drink more coffee

BY PATTI HAGAN

I am a gardenia *appassionata*, having been smit at birth by a whiff of *Gardenia jasminoides* in my native Hawaii. Ever since departing my first garden there, I have tried to lead a gardenia-accessible life. It has not been easy.

Over the years, in sundry overheated, undersunned New York City caves, I have killed scores of gardenias. After each gardeniacide I would wait a decent interval and then, ever the Sisyphean gardener, buy another. I would cart it home in full bud, Proustily expectant of the first redolent waft of benzyl acetate-styrolyl acetate-linalool-linalyl acetate-terpineol-methyl-anthranilate — Gardenia Absolute. Within days the fat green buds would yellow, brown off and drop off: the gardenia would drop dead.

During the '80s I tried self-help in re gardenias. I consulted Thalassa Cruso's *Making Things Grow*. Ms. Cruso began by aspersion: gardenias behave like "temperamental prima donnas" and "only children." She continued by confession: "I am one of those people who can do nothing with gardenias." Then, after declaring "advice about gardenias indoors is very hard to give," she gave her best: "I don't think a novice should spend money buying such a tricky plant."

Regardless, I pushed on to T.H. Everett, the New York Botanical Garden's late horticultural sachem. He turned out to be an unmitigated gardenia disparagist. In his epic *NYBG Illustrated Encyclopedia of Horticulture* (1981), Mr. Everett dismissed gardenias peremptorily: "They are not good houseplants. Their environmental requirements are too exacting"; they will "deteriorate and eventually die." Liberty Hyde Bailey, in his *Standard Cyclopedia of Horticulture* (1933) wrote that despite the gardenia's mid-19th-century rep as "one of the finest stove shrubs in cultivation...it is one of the most difficult plants to handle."

Whenever I get really desperate for plant info I call the Bronx and ask for Lothian Lynas*. A crack English research librarian, Mrs. Lynas is the New York Botanical Garden Library's Miss Marple. So I called her about gardenias. Exactly who was the gardenia's Alexander Garden? Besides Billie Holiday, who wore them in her hair so much they became her trademark, was there an American angle to the gardenia? Within the hour Mrs. Lynas phoned with the particulars on Dr. Garden (1730-91): Scotland-born physician; 30 years resident in Charleston, South Carolina; went back to Britain in 1782 upon confiscation of his newly American property, he having remained an English Loyalist during the Revolution; naturalist; fellow of the Royal Society; friend and correspondent of naturalist John Ellis. Ellis and Garden both corresponded with the Swedish botanist, Carolus Linnaeus, and each petitioned Linnaeus to name a plant for the other. Mrs. Lynas reported, "Some miserable little plant — *Ellisia nyctelea* — got named for Ellis, while the gardenia went on to glory." The American angle, pre-Lady Day's jazz immortalization of the flower as camouflage for a cigarette burn in her hair, Ms. Lynas related, was that in 1760, Linnaeus had grudgingly bestowed Alexander Garden's name on a deliriously fragrant plant recently introduced to England from the Far East, *while Dr. Garden was still resident in colonial America.* Linnaeus groused that by calling a gardenia a gardenia he was "sacrificing science for friendship," and peeved, "I cannot but forsee that this measure will be exposed to much censure," considering, "the ill-natured objections, often made against me, that I name plants after my friends, who have not publicly contributed to the advancement of science." Mrs. Lynas noted that Dr. Garden certainly had not contributed to the advancement of gardenia cultural science. Of two gardenias sent Dr. Garden in 1762, one was DOA and the other died within a year. A despondent Dr. Garden wrote Ellis that the gardenia's "sudden death I take to be no good omen for the continuance and duration of my botanical name and character."

Mrs. Lynas invited me up to vet the NYBG's Gardenia File, a folder filled with many not altogether good-natured objections to the gardenia's captious character by all manner of garden griot. "A most cantankerous house plant...Gardenias can make the most secure gardener nervous" (Linda Yang). "A more finicky flower couldn't have been found" (Tovah Martin). "I might as well warn you right now that gardenias...are mean plants to handle" (Anonymous). "The world's most frustrating house plants...finicky and fractious in a living room" (Jeanne Goode). Indeed, Ms. Goode's

---

* Lothian Lynas retired in 1991 and returned to England.

79

gardenia, "a plant that is almost always suffering," sounds like a real plant martyr. "More symptoms of distress can appear on a gardenia in a week than most plants display in a lifetime. These plants rebel in most houses." Furthermore, "gardenias are intolerant of mistakes and resent change." So who'd want to live with one? "There are no remedies, just things you can do wrong." Clearly, I was unsuited to the gardenia's conservative and imperious lifestyle. Aside from the standard admonitions to keep up "atmospheric humidity" ("gardenias grow best in a rain-forest-type climate") and acidity ("applications of sulfur") and recommendations for "good, hard syringing" with "plain water," no gardenia sage advised anything beyond what I was already doing, or offered much hope of placating the plants.

My gardenia enlightenment happened two years ago, on the day another of my plants gave up the gardenia ghost. A good gardenia-growing friend from high-rise Manhattan, Edith Chang, dropped off her gardenias for the summer in my Brooklyn garden. Quite emphatically she declared that what gardenias really need is to drop acid fairly often. Mind you, not just the occasional hit of Miracid, but everyday break-fast acid: COFFEE GROUNDS! At the time I was trying to kick the coffee habit. For the sake of my gardenia futures I now had good reason not to. Instead, I began mixing a morning slurry of Italian dark roast espresso grounds and using it to top off the daily gardenia watering with an acid chaser. (At the same time I made rain-forest-sure that the cachepot beneath each gardenia held at least 1 1/2 inches of plain water for daylong pseudo-tropical humidification and soil moisturizing.)

I also became an obsessive pest inspector, joining battalions of ladybugs, green lacewings and praying mantises on routine patrol of the plants for scale, mealy bug and red spider mite — pests that love gardenias as much as I do. (Lacewings and mantises even like to lay their eggs on gardenias.) The only other gardenia requisites seemed to be a bright, sunny indoor winter pot spot and five months' summering al fresco. (Even the New York City out-of-doors tones up the plants fast.) Two weeks of fresh-air camp and the gardenias are flush with buds and shiny new leaves.

Coffee grounds have made the critical difference in my relations with these notoriously difficult plants. I haven't offed a gardenia since 1988. Which makes me wonder why coffee is never suggested in gardenia-coddling instructions. Could it be fear of some obscure botanical incest taboo? Both gardenia and coffee are members of the Rubiaceae family, subfamily Cinchonoideae.

My java jive to other gardenia placators: do not hesitate to ply the gardenia with the grounds of its near relation, *Coffea*. Share the extended family acidity. By the strength of strong coffee grounds I've brought two gardenias back from the brink, nourished one scrawny three-inch mail-order cutting to flourishing stove-shrub size

Billie Holiday immortalized gardenias in jazz and America, by wearing — not growing — them.

and rehabilitated one massive mealy bug-mauled plant. In the New York City rain-forest this summer, the gardenias of Gotham have performed spectacularly.

Elvin McDonald, author and houseplant aficionado, once observed: "So many writers have cast an aura of mystery about the gardenia and its culture that gardeners sometimes lose all common sense handling the plant." He admonished: "Approached calmly, gardenia culture is not any more complicated than that of such common plants as the African violet, begonia and geranium." Happily becalmed amid my gardenias I might add: gardenias are easy to grow given an acid enough approach.

This article first appeared in the *The Wall Street Journal* on September 13, 1990. It is reprinted with the permission of the author.

Orchids

In their tropical habitats,
orchids thrive side by side with such commonly grown
houseplants as bromeliads and begonias.
An avid collector tells how to make them thrive on your
windowsills, too

BY CHARLES MARDEN FITCH

rowing tropical orchids in your bright windows is a challenge worth pursuing. In their tropical habitats, orchids thrive side by side with such commonly grown houseplants as bromeliads, begonias, philodendrons and jungle cactus. Orchids will grow equally well in your home once you understand their basic needs.

If you've never grown orchids, begin with mature, established plants.
Above is *Phalaenopsis* Marion Fowler.

In my collection, orchids grow well in bright living room and photo studio windows. In the basement, seedlings and compact orchids grow under broad-spectrum fluorescent lights. From June to September, many of my mature orchids sojourn outside on raised benches or on a terrace table where bright light, abundant fresh air and summer rains encourage sturdy growth.

HOW TO BEGIN

If you are new to orchid growing, begin with mature, established plants, preferably from a nursery where your questions will be answered by experts. Occasionally, flowering dendrobium and phalaenopsis orchids appear on sale at supermarkets, but it is a rare produce manager that is capable of supplying the detailed information that you need to grow the plants.

Specialists at orchid nurseries will be pleased and equipped to answer your questions. I recommend buying established plants rather than attempting the complicated and time-consuming process of growing orchids from seed. Most orchids must be five or six years old before making their first flowers indoors. Although raising small seedlings is slightly easier, it's still not a wise venture for beginners.

Starting with mature plants offers the advantage of instant flowers when you select orchids in bloom or bud at a nursery. In addition, established plants will tolerate occasional cultural mistakes. Mature orchids with well-developed water-storing stems (pseudobulbs) can endure weeks without watering. Larger plants are also more adaptable to variations in humidity and light.

IDEAL INDOOR CONDITIONS

Many tropical orchids do well with 50 to 60 percent relative humidity, a nighttime temperature range of 50 to 70° F, bright diffuse light and good air circulation. Orchid seedlings in general do better with warmer, moister conditions than mature plants. If you provide these conditions, an abundant array of orchid genera will grow for you.

Orchids can be divided into groups according to their preferred nighttime temperatures. The most popular group thrives with nights between 60 and 65° F. A second group, called cold-preference orchids, does best with cool 50 to 60° F nights. This group includes standard-sized cymbidiums, masdevallias, odontoglossums, many laelias, green-leaved paphiopedilums and any orchid species native to high altitudes in the tropics. A third category includes orchids that perform best with warm 68 to 70° F nights, such as most vandas and their hybrids, phalaenopsis, paphiopedilums with mottled leaves and other genera found in tropical lowlands.

Hybrid orchids are generally more adaptable to environmental differences than pure species. Most adaptable of all are the complex hybrids in large-flowering genera bred for vigor, floriferousness and flower quality. This group includes hundreds of cattleya hybrids, cymbidiums, dendrobiums, vandas, ascocentras, paphiopedilums, phalaenopsis and oncidiums. With all these varied orchids from which to choose, you're sure to find several that fit your taste and growing conditions.

Green-leaved paphiopedilums, such as *Paphiopedilum* Niobe, above, a tropical lady slipper orchid, do best with cool, 50 to 60° F nights.

PROVIDING A SUITABLE ENVIRONMENT

For maximum success, create airy, humid growing spaces in front of your brightest windows. I use plastic trays and window boxes with an inch of white gravel at the bottom. The gravel is kept moist to create a locally humid atmosphere. Another useful technique is to fill waterproof trays or windowboxes with several inches of water, then set the orchid pots on plastic, metal, or wooden grids resting over the water-filled containers. If you choose this method, be sure your windowsill or shelf is sufficiently sturdy to withstand the weight.

To further foster humidity, surround the potted orchids with foliage plants and other tropicals such as bromeliads. If the local humidity is still below 50 percent consider adding a small electric humidifier. The type that attaches directly to a water pipe is most convenient — small portable units may need refilling several times a week. Meanwhile, keep air circulating with a small fan aimed at a nearby wall or the ceiling.

LIGHT INTENSITY

In their tropical habitats, some orchids grow in full sun, while other species of the same genus may prefer shady situations. In general, orchids with thick, waxy leaves need bright light whereas those with thin foliage need less intense light. Of the popular cultivated orchids, vanda hybrids, epidendrums and many dendrobiums need the brightest light while cattleyas, oncidiums and cymbidiums do best with diffused light at midday but direct sun in early morning or late afternoon. Phalaenopsis, paphiopedilums and odontoglossums will blossom with medium light — that is, in a bright window where no direct sun hits the leaves except very early or late in the day.

To prevent sunburn, move orchids into brighter light gradually, or shade them during midday when the sun is most intense. Orchids in bloom may be displayed under low light conditions for several weeks without harming the plant. Just remember to provide bright light when new growth begins. Orchids grown with insufficient light have deep green foliage but seldom bloom. Plants given too much light are yellow-green and may develop burned patches.

GROWTH STYLES

Indoor orchids are either epiphytic (adapted to growing in the wild on trees and mossy rocks) or terrestrial (adapted to living in well-drained soil). Orchids I study in their tropical habitats actually show a range of perch preferences varying from bare tree bark or hard clean rock to gravelly soil or humus along stream banks. Similarly, orchids in cultivation succeed in many different potting mixtures. Epiphytic orchids such as cattleyas and epidendrums thrive in rapidly draining mixtures of tree fern or fir bark with charcoal, coarse perlite and similar ingredients. The terrestrial (or ground-dwelling) genera such as cymbidiums and paphiopedilums need a finer mixture that holds more moisture but still has excellent drainage. When you buy your first orchids, be sure to ask the professional grower to recommend a suitable potting mixture. In my collection, I use a base mix of tree fern or fir bark with hardwood charcoal and coarse perlite (volcanic rock). If the orchid needs more moisture, I add coarse New Zealand sphagnum moss or employ a smaller grade of bark or tree fern. Some of my orchids do well with a base mixture of ground cork but the cork tends to decompose in 15 to 20 months. Repot orchids when they outgrow their container or when the mixture deteriorates. Fully rotten potting mix holds too much moisture and will encourage root rot.

CHOOSING POTS

For terrestrials and smaller epiphytic genera, I like plastic pots with extra drainage holes. One design (the Rand aircone pot) has an inner central cone with air holes allowing the center of a filled pot to receive air movement. However, large orchids tend to be unstable in plastic pots and they should be given heavy clay containers.

For success with orchids, create airy, humid growing spaces in front of your brightest windows. Above is *Brassolaeliocattleya* 'Talisman Cove'.

Special clay pots are available with extra side drainage holes especially designed for epiphytic orchids. Repot orchids when new growth begins, usually in spring and summer. Avoid disturbing roots during blooming or resting periods.

Increase drainage and air circulation by using an inch or two of coarse gravel, hardwood charcoal, or styrofoam "peanuts" in the bottom of each pot. Add an inch of potting mix, then spread the plant's roots over the mix and gradually tuck in more of the growing medium, occasionally tapping the pot on a hard surface to settle the mix around the roots as you work. Before trying to pot or transplant your first orchid, it's wise to watch an experienced grower perform the procedure.

MOUNTED PLANTS

In environments where humidity is high, equitant oncidiums (dwarf oncidiums with succulent, often grooved, leaves), smaller encyclias and many other miniature epiphytic orchids can be successfully grown mounted on slabs of bark, tree fern or cork. However, bear in mind that mounted plants usually require more attention because they dry out rapidly.

WATERING

Orchids with pseudobulbs can live for weeks without root watering if the atmospheri humidity is high. In fact, a common cause of orchid mortality is overwatering. Eve terrestrial orchids must have good air circulation around the roots. Too much mois ture, especially when plants are not making rapid growth, often leads to root rot.

Clear plastic pots, such as the Rand type, or clay pots with extra side drainag holes are ideal because you can readily observe the moisture level of the mix. After few seasons of experience, you will know how often different orchids need waterin, under your growing conditions. Factors that influence how often your orchids nee water include: relative humidity, light intensity, air circulation, formula of the pottin mix, type of pot used and the growth stage of each plant.

How do you tell when an orchid needs water? If the orchid in question ha pseudobulbs, watch the plumpness of the bulbs just behind the active growth (th newly forming pseudobulb). When the mature pseudobulb begins to shrink (that is it develops slight grooves) it is safe to soak the roots. For plants in clay pots, I ta each pot with my ring or fingernail. A light hollow sound indicates a dry potting mix a thud means the mix is moist. Lifting a pot to judge its weight is also useful. Lear how to judge by lifting pots just after watering, then compare the weight several day later when the medium is dry. In clear plastic pots, you can easily observe the mois ture of the roots. Dry roots are white, wet roots are green or gray.

WHICH ORCHIDS?

How do you choose which orchids to grow? Aesthetics is as good a basis for choosin as any. If you love cattleya type flowers, then cattleya hybrids should fill your win dows. Within popular orchid groups, you can find hybrids that fit both your prefer ences and conditions. Visiting local orchid shows and orchid greenhouses will help yo learn about different genera.

LEARNING MORE

The best way to continue to learn more about orchids is to join the American Orchi Society. New members receive a free culture handbook. A most important monthl benefit is the colorful *A.O.S. Bulletin*. Articles feature growing information, ne trends in hybridizing and profiles of orchids. Advertisements offer supplies and plant from dealers in many countries. For a free membership leaflet write:
American Orchid Society • 6000 South Olive Ave. • West Palm Beach, Fl 33405-4159

Water Does Not Mean Love

In hot, dry rooms where most houseplants languish,

some succulent is sure to thrive

BY LINDA YANG

"I f in doubt let them do without" seems to be the motto of those who grow cacti and other succulents. No, these are not a callous group of plant haters. They are perfectly nice people who have learned to control what seems to be a natural inclination when it comes to houseplants — that is, equating love with water.

Zabel Meshejian, president of the New York Chapter of The Cactus and Succulent Society, waters once a week. And she has learned that nothing dire happens when her plants are ignored for two weeks.

The diverse group of plants known as succulents, a category that includes cacti, has survived by adapting to drought. For this reason, quite a few make good houseplants. In hot, dry rooms, where foliage plants may falter, some succulent is sure to survive — if it isn't killed by an overdose of water.

Succulents such as these living stones (*Lithops* spp.) are adapted to drought.

TOVAH MARTIN

START CHEAP

Don't be embarrassed to start your cacti and succulent collection with the inexpensive plants from dime stores, florists or botanical garden shops. You can't become an expert without making mistakes, and it's better to kill cheap purchases first. You can also order from one of the following specialty mail-order suppliers:

ABBEY GARDENS
4620 Carpinteria Ave.
Carpinteria, CA 93013
Catalog $2 (Refundable with order)

ARID LANDS GREENHOUSES
3560 West Bilby Rd.
Tucson, AZ 85746
Free List

HIGHLANDS SUCCULENTS
1446 Bear Run Rd.
Gallipolis, OH 45631
Catalog $2

RAINBOW GARDENS
1444 East Taylor St.
Vista, CA 92084
Catalog $2

SINGERS' GROWING THINGS
17806 Plummer St.
Northridge, CA 91325
Catalog $1.50 (Refundable with order).

Then, too, there's nothing like hobnobbing with gardeners with similar interests. For information on the Cactus and Succulent Society of America, Inc., write to Mindy Fusaro, OOB 35034, Des Moines, IA 50315-0301. Yearly dues are $30.

The word succulent is derived from the Latin, *sucus*, and means juicy or fleshy. Although all plants store some water in their roots, stems or leaves, the storage ability of succulents is highly developed.

Succulents include an enormous diversity of species, culled from over 20 families. Many have grotesque or bizarre looking swollen trunks, stems or leaves. In effect, they're the plant world's equivalent of the camel. Indeed, it is precisely because of their extraordinary sculptural forms – ugly, weird and beautiful – that so many find them endlessly fascinating.

Although Ms. Meshejian has experimented with many kinds in the past decade, her present passion is the group known as caudiciforms, succulents with trunks swollen at the base where water and nutrients are stored. Included are the wildly sculpted elephant's foot (*Dioscorea elephantipes*), whose segmented bark has corrugated, angled

Sansevierias, leathery-looking members of the lily family, are easy to grow.

knobs out of which springs a thin stalk with heart-shaped leaves and chartreuse flowers, and the more graceful desert rose (*Adenium obesum*) whose fleshy, twisted branches bear thick green and pink leaves and rose-colored flowers.

According to Bill Ballard, co-owner of Highland Succulents, a nursery in Gallipolis, Ohio, people often start buying these plants strictly on the basis of their peculiar looks. And then they make the mistake of watering incorrectly. It's important to understand the plants' natural life cycles, according to Mr. Ballard. And this is a function of the plants' native habitats.

In autumn, for example, plants native to South Africa or the Canary Islands are preparing for summer, and thus are entering a period of active growth. So this is the time to begin regular watering of plants like the dragon-tree aloe (*Aloe dichotoma*), which has thick, silvery green-edged, barbed leaves,

Many succulents have striking, sculptural forms. Above is *Crassula simsii*.

and *Euphorbia atropurpurea*, which has narrow, silvery blue foliage. Regular watering for these winter growers means moisture once a week or so, depending on the room's heat and light.

Succulents entering a period of growth in autumn can also be treated to a monthly solution of a diluted, all-purpose fertilizer. On the other hand, in autumn, plants native to Central America and Southwestern United States are preparing for winter, and thus are entering a period of rest. So, this is the time to stop watering cacti like the old man (*Cephalocereus senilis*) which is shrouded in what appears to be long white hairs, or *Mammillaria elegans*, which is covered by short, sharp spines.

Asterophytum myriostigma and other succulents require a fast-draining soil.

Plants entering a dormant period should be neglected — just short of the point at which they begin to shrivel, according to Lem Higgs, owner of Abbey Garden Cacti and Succulent Nursery in Carpinteria, California. As a general rule, these plants need water once a month or so through autumn, and then in December and January once every six weeks or so. Sometime between February and April, increase watering to every other week, because that is the beginning of their period of growth.

A fast-draining soil is also essential. A basic soil blend suggested by Mr. Higgs for most succulents is 70 percent perlite or pumice and a 30 percent combination of ground fir bark, peat moss, leaf mold and other composted organic matter.

At one time, Manny Singer and his wife Bert collected succulents from the wild. But since too many of these plants have become endangered, the couple now propagate unusual species from seeds and cuttings at their Northridge, California, nursery, Singers' Growing Things.

Mature plants that are rare and weird can be quite expensive. For example, the *Bursera microphylla*, which resembles a wind-blown bonsai, sells for over $200 at Singers' Growing Things. "I must offer condolences to people who start with plants like these and don't know what they're doing," says Mr. Singer.

He suggests that beginners start with plants such as haworthias, many of which sell for under $5. This group, which includes several hundred species, are typically small, fleshy-leaved plants whose plump foliage is arranged in a star shape called a sette. Among the common names applied to some haworthias are the pearl-plant and zebra haworthia. These are apt descriptions of the pearl-like dots on the leaves that are sometimes spaced so closely they resemble stripes.

Although succulents are often associated with heat and sun, haworthias are among the species in this extraordinarily varied group that actually prefer some shade. Two to three hours of sunlight daily is fine for *Haworthia truncata, H. maughanii, H. retusa* and *H. cooperi*, for example.

Even less sunlight — just a brightly lit room — will also suffice for a number of sansevierias, another huge group of succulents collectively known as snake plants. Sansevierias are leathery looking members of the lily family whose elongated, upright silver, green or gold foliage comes in assorted stripes or mottled patterns. Some sansevierias have long, cylindrical leaves, while others are short and squat and look like bird's nests.

CHARLES MARDEN FITCH

Hoyas require less light than other succulents. Above is *Hoya carnosa*.

Also surprising are the cacti that do not like sun, do not grow in the desert and have no markedly prickly spines. These are the tree perchers, or epiphytic jungle cacti. Chuck Everson, owner of Rainbow Gardens in Vista California, is especially fond of this group of succulents, which are also known as orchid cacti.

Many orchid cacti have graceful cascading limbs that make them ideal for hanging baskets. Best known are the Christmas and Thanksgiving cacti, whose blooms are borne on flattened, segmented stems. There are quite a few new hybrids, according to Mr. Everson, including one called 'Bridgeport', which has pure white flowers and upright, rather than pendulous stems, and 'Santa Cruz', whose large flowers are peach and white.

Also useful for low-light sills are the hoyas, another group of pendulous succulents. One easily grown species, the sweetheart hoya (*H. kerrii*) has heart-shaped leaves and peculiar, flattened, globe-shaped blooms in summer.

As winter approaches, be stingy when watering these plants. But how do you know exactly how much to add? "Stick your finger into the soil down past the first joint," Mr. Everson suggests. "If there's no moisture, it's probably time to add some — I guess you could say this is a rule of thumb that sometimes works."

Adapted from an article that first appeared in *The New York Times*.

Index

COMMON NAMES

BBG Gardening Guides